The
Scots
and their
Fish

The Scots and their Fish

Wallace Lockhart

Birlinn

First published in Great Britain, 1997, by
Birlinn Limited
14 High Street
Edinburgh EH1 1TE

© Wallace Lockhart, 1997

The moral right of the author has been asserted.

British Library Cataloguing-in-Publication Data
A Catalogue record of this book is available
from the British Library.

ISBN 1 874744 81 5

Designed and typeset in 10.5/12pt Berkeley
by Janet Watson

Made and printed in Finland by
Werner Söderström OY

Contents

Acknowledgements

My first expression of thanks must go to those fishermen of many years ago who so kindly tolerated the presence of a young boy holding the mistaken conviction he could be of some use to them around their boats. At least, from an early age, I became aware of the physical and social demands the sea makes on those who pursue her harvest.

For filling in gaps in my knowledge I am obliged to some very committed individuals. Jim Lindsay and his staff at the Scottish Fisheries Museum at Anstruther gave me with the greatest willingness, access to books and documents, pictures and technical comment. To the Sea Fish Authority I am also indebted; for providing me with material and recipes and arranging for me to visit the Authority's research station at Acharacle. Skipper Robert Ross of Tarbert, Fisheries Officer Duncan McGregor at Oban, Murdo MacDonald of Argyll and Bute District Council, Donny McLeod, harbourmaster at Ullapool have all added to my knowledge, while my old friend Harry Knox of British Rail reminded me of the great fish trains of yesteryear. And for pulling together some loose ends, my appreciation goes to Mrs E. Findlay of the Arbuthnot Museum at Peterhead and George Pirie, harbourmaster at Whitehills.

That the sea is in our blood can be seen clearly by the amount of literature that abounds on the subject. For the giving of permission to quote the following poem and prose passages I express my sincere thanks.

Naomi Mitchison for 'The Alban Goes Out'.

Angus Martin for 'Bait Gathering' and 'Limpets'.

Reed Books for 'In Scotland Again' by H.V. Morton.

Derik S. Thomson for 'The Herring Girls' contained in his Collection *Creachadh na Clàrsaich/Plundering the Harp*.

George Bruce for 'The Fisherman' and 'Tom on the Beach'.

Allie Windwick for 'Partans in his Creel'.

The estate of the late George Mackay Brown for 'Old Fisherman with Guitar' and 'Greenvoe', published by John Murray Ltd.

Lillian Grant Rich for 'Foghorn in the Night'.

Introduction

Some think of the fisher skipper
Beyond the Inchcape stone
But I of the fisher woman
That lies at home alone.

'I Sit Up Here at Midnight',
Robert Louis Stevenson

Every Tuesday we had smokies for tea. Huge golden-skinned masses of white flesh which filled the frying pan and oozed juices worthy of the gods. Truth to tell, we ate smokies on more days than Tuesday. But Tuesday's meal was as well defined as church on Sunday. For on Tuesday morning came the Arbroath fish-wife, red of cheek and ample of bosom, her cheery face fostering friendship with every house in turn. Apron-clad, her blue and white striped skirt and blue blouse imaged the sea and its followers. The monstrous basket on her back, its weight borne by a stretch of webbing across her shoulders, indicated the strength of her body. As she sold her fish from house to house, she and her kind were as much a part of the world as the 'bobby' on the beat.

To a youngster growing up in the east of Scotland in an earlier age, smokies were not one's only contact with fish. The word 'scampi' had not yet entered the vocabulary but the pursuit of dabs and podlies filled many a school

ix

holiday. To see the fishing boats come in was always a thrill and many a crab which had mistakenly found its way into a net was tossed to the youngster hoping to be admitted to the wheelhouse after the catch had been landed and the boat made ready for the next day. Mussels, I remember, we ignored apart from using them as bait, but whelks, or 'buckies' as we called them, were occasionally plucked from the rocks and taken home and boiled. Then, with pin in hand, the body was speared out. I have a feeling we did not enjoy them overmuch, they had a connotation of the French eating frogs and snails, something which appeared revolting. Dulse, the long brown seaweed, would occasionally be chewed although I think it was the excitement of seeing and smelling it being roasted with a red hot poker rather than its actual flavour that encouraged the taste buds to lubricate. Neil Gunn's *Morning Tide* had not yet entered my ken:

> *The tangle was not so hard as a bone, but very nearly.*
> *But the bit he broke off was sweet and tender to his palate,*
> *and its saline flavour excited a greater flow of spittle than*
> *ever so that his mouth moved richly and he swallowed*
> *many times. A tangle was always a little disappointing in*
> *the first minute, as though the memory of it contained more*
> *food. But once you started gnawing you could not stop.*

Fish and chip shop fish were a real treat, especially when there was that guarantee of quality, an Italian name, above the door. Hogmanay brought large-wheeled barrows by the dozen on to the streets, decked high with kippers dressed as dolls in brightly coloured paper. Whatever happened to that custom?

Another memory not to be erased from these early days was the sight of the fish trains thundering down the line. The 'Aberdeen Fish' was a special favourite. Sixty vans in length and travelling up to 75 miles an hour she had a personality of her own. As the vans rocked and rolled, water from the tons of ice she carried to keep the fish fresh washed anyone silly enough not to stand well back from the track. While it might be just a slight exaggeration to say her coming was preceded by her smell, it is no exaggeration to say her passing and after-presence left an odour in the nostrils that only the sadist would wish to inhale again voluntarily. Holding the same rail priority status as express passenger trains, the major fish trains ran on a fixed timetable. The 'Aberdeen Fish' for example left Guild Street Yard every day at 13.43 hours. Nothing was ever allowed to delay its departure and it arrived at King's Cross Goods Yard at one o'clock in the morning. Fish vans were also loaded along the Moray Firth and north-east ports and as far west as Mallaig. From the fishing villages of the East Neuk of Fife up to six trains might be loaded in the height of the herring season. Where a full train load was not available, the part load would be dispatched as tail traffic on passenger trains, such was the importance attached to getting the fish as speedily as possible to its destination. In the 1960s a gentleman by the name of Dr Beeching carrying out a survey of the profitability of rail lines and traffic on behalf of the Government of the day, decreed the fish traffic from Scotland to the south to be uneconomic. In one of the quickest 'kill-offs' in history, a way of life that seemed as secure as an anchor disappeared from the scene and entered legend.

Even at an early age, one was aware that fishing communities were different. Adults talked about 'close brethren' and the singing of fishermen in mission halls; the way the exterior of their houses seemed to sparkle because of their white-washed or painted walls; their lifeboat service; and their habit of only marrying within their own communities; until they almost seemed a race apart. And when one stood on the pier watching the tiniest of boats leave harbour to succumb to motions that would not have disgraced a fairground tummy tumbler, admiration for their skills was mixed with gratitude and relief one was on dry land. As the foam broke over the bow and the blue-clad figures set about their work, the words of Tennyson lingered in the mind:

And may there be no moaning of the bar
When I put out to sea.

'Crossing the Bar'

There were other fishing boats that could lure small boys. Hours could be passed watching the salmon cobbles at work, waiting with ever-increasing excitement to see how many fish had been caught in the sweep. The seeming miles of nets, stretching along the beaches and into the breakers, were apparently erected for the climbing enjoyment of small boys, an idea not shared by the weatherbeaten characters sitting in the bothy waiting for the tide to go out. In later life, a holiday by the sea meant putting out one's own creel for lobster and crab and, less pleasantly, discovering the horrific extent of nylon gill netting round our coasts.

At school I was taught English for a while by George Bruce. He hailed from the north-east tip of land we call 'Buchan', that land of 'nine months winter and three months "coorse" weather'. I was vaguely aware that he wrote poetry although he modestly refrained from introducing his pupils to his own work. A pity, because his poetry reminds us of where gulls cry from the clouds and where salt lies on the leaves of trees as in, 'The Fisherman':

> As he comes from one of those small houses
> Set within the curve of the low cliff
> For a moment he pauses
> Foot on step at the low lintel
> Before fronting wind and sun.
> He carries out from within something of the dark
> Concealed by heavy curtain,
> Or held within the ship under hatches.

If the poetry of George Bruce made its penetration through the senses, I found the travel writer I loved so well, H.V. Morton, was master of letting the picture tell the story. Having gone to sea on an Aberdeen trawler, his reporting in *In Scotland Again* needed no embellishing to make me appreciate the fish on my plate:

> 'Skipper wants you on the bridge,' shouted someone;
> and I staggered forward, with the sea hissing by and the
> trawler's nose now high in the air and now deep in the
> trough of the swell.

The wheel-house rose high above the deck and its windows rattled like the windows of an elderly taxi cab. The skipper stood with one arm flung in a friendly way over the wheel. A compass swung from the roof, but there were no maps or charts. 'Don't need 'em,' said the skipper. 'Been on the North Sea for fifty year.'

At one time it was considered bad form to talk about food. Nowadays, some people talk about little else. But there is little doubt advancing years bring with them a greater interest in and appreciation of what lands before us on the table. When scampi and prawn cocktails became food for everyone I have absolutely no recollection. It seems as if one day they were unknown items and the next day they were commonplace dishes we had never lived without. The same cannot be said about my introduction to 'Sole Betty Lou' – whatever happened to 'Sole Betty Lou'? In the late Fifties, specialist fish restaurants were in spate; they were opening up all over the place. As a gauche young man I crossed the portals of the 'Fisherman's Wharf' in Kensington. The price of a meal would have kept a drifter at sea for a week. But the menu! Every conceivable fish in amalgam with every conceivable accompaniment.

My purse rose to 'Sole Betty Lou'. What sophistication! A Dover sole topped with fried banana and sweet corn. What I had for lunch yesterday I cannot remember. But 'Sole Betty Lou' lingers with me like 'Calais' on Queen Mary's heart.

Today the fishing industry is beset with problems. The sea has been overfished for too many years and stocks have been savaged. To compete, fishermen have had to invest in ever-more expensive boats and gear. Leglislation to restrict their days at sea will, one hopes, result in fish stocks rising. But the restricted fishing time being allowed is making it difficult for the present fishermen to make a livelihood and repay loans on their boat and equipment investments. Changes to net sizes have had mixed success. The trawl is not a selective item when it comes to types of fish entering its mouth. To make matters worse, there are difficulties with rights to fish in cetain places and there are accusations of illegal practices by fishermen from other Common Market countries. The need for wisdom to sort out the conflict that faces us never been greater.

Fish have fortified the Scots since time well beyond our ken. In this little book I have tried to give background and interest to the beguiling object which, naked or packaged enters our shopping creel to satisfy our wants. And if this book contains a hidden agenda, let it be that it is to make us more appreciative of those who toil with nets far from our shores.

1

Ports, Boats and Fisherfolk

Here, in this little Bay,
Full of tumultuous life and great repose,
Where, twice a day,
The purposeless, glad ocean comes and goes,
Under high cliffs, and far from the huge towns,
I sit me down.
from 'To the Unknown Eros', Book I: XII, *Magna ést Veritas*,
C.K.D. Patmore

Fishing villages decorate the coast of Scotland in an apparently haphazard way. Often it seems their positioning is devoid of logic, as, for example, when they are sited at the foot of a cliff like Auchmithie near Arbroath or Gardenstoun on the Banff coast, up which catch and tackle must be manhandled. But the fisherman's eyes are not those of the landsman's. And while it is true many fishing communities took root where they did because of landlord pressure, most developed in accordance with the value set upon the location in terms of shelter from the weather, easy beaching conditions and a plentiful supply of bait. Their initial smallness and proliferation points to their origins being family based. Even today in those hamlets which have grown into towns, a flip through the 'phone book will show the strength of tribal names. Try counting all the Swankies and Cargills in Arbroath.

Although frequently close together, the separate identities of the communities serve to emphasise their independence. Look at the few miles that separate Montrose and Stonehaven. Yet from that small strip of land, boats of one sort or another go out or have gone out from Milton, Johnshaven, Gourdon, Shieldhill, Catterline and Crawton. Similarly, along the Banff and Buchan coast the villages of Portknockie, Findochty, Portlessie, Cullen and Rosehearty are only some of the twenty-odd villages that snuggle into the thirty-odd miles of coastline between Fraserburgh and Buckie. Records for some of these settlements go back before the seventeenth century. One might have expected the rich fishing grounds of the Firth of Forth to have fostered the growth of one major fishing city, but again there is proliferation: Leven, Largo, St Monans, Pittenweem, Anstruther, Cellardyke and Crail ring the Fife coastline with the cosiest of harbours. Writing around the turn of the century, Sir Archibald Geikie in his *Scottish Reminiscences* enthused madly about this coastline:

> On the east side of the kingdom it has long been noted how tenaciously the fisher folk cling to their old habits and customs. Red-tiled, corby-stepped houses, thrusting their gables into the street, climbing one above another up the steep slope that rises from the beach, and crowned by the picturesque old church or town hall with its quaint spire, give a picturesqueness to the shores of the Forth such as no other part of the coastline can boast. Then the little harbours with their fleets of strong fishing boats, rich brown sails, 'hard coils of cordage, swarthy fishing nets', and piles of barrels and baskets, bear witness to the staple industry of the inhabitants. The women may be seen sitting in groups at their doors, mending the nets or baiting the nets for the next night's fishing. Such places as St Monans, Pittenweem, Anstruther, Crail and St Andrews, afford endless subjects for the artist.

Distinct communities, of course, develop characteristics and one can think of two reasons right away that explain how fishing places have their reputation for closeness.

First, the whole community had to become geared to serving the fishermen. Wives and children gathered mussels for the lines they would bait. Smoking the fish in the main was women's work so it becomes easy to understand how marriage outwith the community was frowned upon. The culture shock to any innocent girl being introduced to the non-stop work of a fisherman's wife must have been horrific. Second, tragedy brings people together and fishing has a history of tragedy. Even today with the steady release of weather news, radar and other navigational aids, the sea takes its toll of men and ships. Fishing communities have long memories. How can the people of Eyemouth forget the disaster of 1881 when one-hundred and twenty-nine of their men perished only eight miles from the shore in a freak storm? The same sea laps the harbour wall today.

It does not seem that fishermen were subjected to as much cruelty as crofters during the Clearances. (Many Highlanders of course were resettled on coastal strips where they had to adapt to a new mode of life or go under.) This is not to suggest fisherfolk did not have problems with their overlords. Holders of Crown charters held possession of 'Fishings, hawkings and huntings' and we know that many fishermen were obliged to hand over part of their catch to their overlord. A feudal due of one night's fishing a week was common. The court book of the Barony of Urie in Kincardineshire tells us fishermen in the seventeenth century were obliged to pay a yearly custom to the laird's lady of a hundred haddock and a pint of oil. Not so blessed was the superior of David Straton in Angus. Straton, rather than hand over his obligatory tenth salmon, threw every tenth one back into the sea proclaiming with a martyr's zeal that the superior could fish for them himself. Over on the west coast the Duke of Argyll was more fortunate. In 1663 he secured a tack or lease of the dues on all the herring caught on the western seaboard from the Pentland Firth to the Mull of Galloway.

The crown at least seems long to have recognised the importance of fishing as a national asset. As long ago as

1493 James IV ordered maritime burghs to build vessels for fishing and, incidentally, press all idle persons into service. James V, annoyed at the Dutch fishing in western approaches, tried to settle some Fife fishermen on the Outer Hebrides. The islanders however preferred the Dutch and sent the Fife settlers packing. George I assented to an Act of Parliament in 1718 which gave fishermen a bounty on their catch. This bounty had a long life, not being abolished until 1830. By this time, the Napoleonic wars being over, fishing was flourishing, and large ports like Fraserburgh and Macduff were rising to national prominence.

One of the most beautifully sited ports in Scotland, and one with an interesting recent history, is Ullapool in Wester Ross. For many years Ullapool played second fiddle to Mallaig as the main west coast port for herring landings. Indeed, according to legend, at one time a herring tail was never seen to twinkle in the waters of Loch Broom because of the activities of Lewis witches. The Ullapool men however came up with the answer. They made a silver herring, and towing it behind them in the Minch, they enticed the shoals to follow them into Loch Broom where they allowed the silver herring to take up residence. Success has since been theirs.

Subsequent over-fishing of the Minch resulted in a five-year ban on fishing being instituted. When the ban was lifted in the late 1970s the public's taste for herring was waning, but to save the day there arrived the 'Klondykers', ships from other countries inhibited from fishing Scottish waters by international leglislation but keen to buy for their own countries' consumption. Although frequently thought of as Russian ships, the 'Klondykers' in fact come from many countries. Although the East Europeans provide the bulk of the fleet, ships from Mediterranean countries as far away as Egypt may be present. Incredibly, as many as sixty ships may be involved. As well as buying catches from Scottish fishermen,'Klondykers' are often factory ships, capable in the sheltered waters around Ullapool of processing and canning the fish on board. Recent years have seen mackerel come to the fore as a delicacy and Ullapool has reaped the benefit, thanks to the unlikely combination of nature and leglislation. Mackerel shoals are now moving into Scottish western waters from Shetland later in the year than hitherto. This means the fish are available for catching at the beginning of the calendar year when the boats have their year's catch quota ahead of them. Ullapool is now the leading mackerel port in Scotland; 1992 landings exceeded £6,000,000. Certainly the mackerel landings are concentrated into the early months of the year, but growing shellfish landings, both from local boats and crabbers from the Channel Islands together with Autumn herring landings from the Minches, are helping to spread the port's workload over the year.

In contrast to Ullapool is Oban's story as a fishing port. Oban has never quite made it as a fishing port and one wonders why not? It has one of the most sheltered harbours on the west coast, as well as slipways and ample berthage. Certainly it is a substantial holiday resort but there is nothing incompatible in the combination of fishing port and holiday resort. Many resorts such as Aberdeen, Arbroath and Scarborough provide such proof. Indeed it could be argued that holidaymakers find the watching of boats unloading their catches as pleasant a way of passing time as any. So, what is the fishing story of this gloriously sited town?

A sift through the Oban Town Council minutes of the last century shows little concentration on fishing issues. Not that the Council officers were devoid of a normal desire to make their mark. *A Regulation for the Good Government and Police of the Burgh* of the 22nd December 1822 advises:

> *That the practice of leaving the heads and entrails of fish upon the shores and in the neighbourhood of the streets and houses to putrify there, ought to be put a stop to as offensive and prejudicial to the cleanliness of the Town and health of its inhabitants.*

Those who didn't heed the injunction to cart the offending bits and pieces away for manuring or other purposes as directed by the Dean of Guild were liable to pay a five-shilling fine. One wonders how seriously this piece of leglislation was taken. A hundred years later the local medical officer was lodging complaint about the shortage of barrels available for the collection of herring guts. Even the august 'Argylshire Gathering' would consider it necessary to formally raise in 1929 the issue of smells in the town.

The railway came to Oban in 1880, bringing, no doubt, a feeling of optimism in some quarters that the town could develop as a fishing port now that swifter access to markets was possible. And there was a measure of success. West coast herring could boast a larger size than their east coast brethren and these larger fish found favour in the American market; smaller fish were sought by the Germans and Russians, their markets being supplied by the ports on the other side of the country. Growth was steady and the peak was reached in 1929 when over 26,000 crans were landed. Then came disaster – the herring stocks started to decline – the boats moved to fish elsewhere. The 8,000 crans landed in 1931 dropped to an almost unbelievable 11 crans in 1936.

Stocks did return after the war but by then markets and public demand were changing. The railway which had opened up trade for Oban was no longer seen in such a friendly light. To quote from a Finance and Law Committee paper:

> . . . the freight of fresh fish to London being over £5 per ton definitely discouraged buyers from remaining on at Oban. In particular the Railway Company insisted that all freight transport required by the industry should be by means of their rail services solely, thus preventing [as permitted at other ports] the buyers shipping direct to the Continent and absolutely forbidding their importation at the beginning of the season of stock, salt and barrels by sea-borne transport.

Today a certain amount of white-fish fishing – haddock, cod and hake – is carried out from Oban by boats from elsewhere. The local fleet now concentrates on the shellfish market and a fine job it makes of it. But still the visitor driving down the road from the north into that most beautiful of bays must feel a sense of unreality that no fleet of seine-netters will welcome his arrival.

While our capital city gives the impression that it has, at least physically turned its back on the Forth (William Powere once commented that the Newhaven fishwife in Edinburgh was like a trader from a foreign land), there is no doubt that the histories of the Forth fishing ports are amongst the best documented. The fishermen on the south side of the river seemed to have been more commercially astute than their counterparts on the other side, or, perhaps they just possessed easier access to markets. Anyway, the Fisherrow boats frequently found it more profitable to take part in 'couping', the buying of fish from East Neuk boats, rather than to fish themselves. And also for a while they restricted the sale of mussels from their rich beds to those Fife boats which would land fish at their ports.

The variety and quantity of fish landed at the East Neuk ports was remarkable. George Gourlay in his, *Memorials of Cellardyke* quotes the Minister of Kilrenny in the mid-eighteenth century:

> *He remembers, he tells us, when the mackerel was fished with success at the doors, and as for cod and ling, he has seen some ten or twelve big boats sailing into harbour loaded to the gunwale, and with perhaps thirty or forty, or even fifty, of the largest cod fastened to a rope and towed at the stern.*

The fishermen of that time, and indeed also in later years, had not only the sea to fear. Gourlay again tells us it is doubtful if anywhere on the Scottish coast was the sea-faring community so cruelly harassed by the pressgang as in the East Neuk of Fife. Fishermen were lifted from the beach as well as being forced from their homes and sobbing families to be put in irons until taken aboard the man o' war needing their services. Horrible as that was, one's fury rises more when it is learned a favourite trick of the press-gang was to wait in hiding for a boat returning from the fishing grounds and grab the crew in their exhausted condition. No wonder the spies who would secretly mark the house of a good seaman were so detested. No wonder secret warning signs were put up by wives when the presence of the press-gang (frequently the worse from drink) was noted. Many a fisherman had a secret recess or bolthole he would make for when there was an unknown knock at the door. John Galt in his book, *The Provost* gives a poignant description of a press-gang at work:

> *I was in a state of horror unspeakable. Then came some three or four of the press-gang with a struggling sailor in their clutches, with nothing but his trousers on – his shirt riven from his back in the fury. Syne came the rest of the gang and their officers, scattered as it were with a tempest of mud and stones, pursued and battered by a troop of desperate women and weans, whose fathers and brothers were in jeopardy. And these were followed by the wailing wife of the pressed man, with her five bairns, clamouring in their agony to heaven against the King and Government for the outrage. I couldna' listen to the fearful justice of their outcry, but sat down in a corner of the council-chamber with my fingers in my ears.*

Despite their hatred of the press-gang, many fishermen did volunteer for occasional service with the colours in the Naval Volunteers when called upon, and the fishers of Fife joined the fleet in large numbers in 1807 to serve under Gambier in seizing the Danish Fleet. Writing about the coast of Fife in later years, Robert Louis Stevenson in his essay, 'Coast of Life', suggests a lingering sense of oppression:

> *History broods over that part of the world like the easterly haar. Of these little towns, posted along the shore as close as sedges, each with its bit of harbour, its old weather beaten church or public building, its flavour of decayed prosperity and decaying fish, not one but has its legend, quaint or tragic.*

In this essay, Stevenson goes on to remind us that Alexander Selkirk, whose exploits prompted the tale of

Robinson Crusoe from Daniel Defoe, hailed from Largo and that Paul Jones, the Scot from Galloway who became the 'father of the American Navy' would sally with his ships of war up the Forth. It is said that when the American fleet was off the coast, the Reverend Mr Shirra from Burntisland had a table carried between tide-marks, and publicly prayed against 'the rover' (Paul Jones) at the pitch of his voice. But the main visitor attraction on the coast today is the Scottish Fisheries Museum at Anstruther. Here, amidst the boats and creels, the sounds and smells and paraphernalia of the sea, the visitor meets the starkness of the fisherman's life head-on. It is an experience not to be missed.

For many years Aberdeen was the undisputed major fishing port in Scotland. History was on her side. Landings can be traced in records back to the thirteenth century and even when Aberdeen boats were not to the fore, boats from other home ports and other countries have sought to use her commercial and rail distribution facilities. Prominent throughout the years of the herring boom, the 'Granite City' also saw service as a leading whaling port until around 1850. As elsewhere, trawling at the end of last century was regarded as a dangerous practice, destroying small fish and spawn, but after the local fishermen adopted the 'if you can't beat them, join them' attitude, progress was swift. According to Gloria Wilson in her *More Scottish Fishing Craft*, by 1902, Aberdeen owned 198 trawlers and was the third trawl port in the UK after Hull and Grimsby. Overfishing of the North Sea combined with the greater catching power of modern ships with all their fancy high technology has seen the inevitable drop in shipping numbers. By 1967 the Aberdeen fleet stood at 114 although landings were on a par with thirty years earlier. Today, Aberdeen has lost its pre-eminence to near-neighbour Peterhead, with, some might argue, a more accommodating berthing policy.

In terms of monetary value and weight of landings, Peterhead today stands supreme. Provisional figures for 1991 indicate £81 million pounds of fish were landed at Peterhead with Aberdeen second at just over £26 million. Lerwick in Shetland comes second in terms of weight landed. Associated with line fishing and whaling, Peterhead was always in the lead in the great herring days. At one time nearly 500 boats were based in the port. Herring continued to be important to Peterhead into the 1950s, longer than most ports, due no doubt to its proximity to the Buchan grounds. Slow to take up seine-netting initially, Peterhead then built up a fleet of motor vessels big enough to undertake long herring trips and capable of seine-netting. Changes in fishing techniques such as purse seine-netting and trawling in pairs for white fish has brought further success.

Fishing today still retains the reputation of being the world's most dangerous occupation. As we sit in the comfort of our homes, it is difficult, if not well-nigh impossible for us to fully appreciate the daily risks and misery that had to be endured in earlier years by line fishermen working in completely open-boat conditions. A hundred years ago boats around twenty-five feet in length with a crew of six were common. These boats would work up to ten miles from land. Although equipped with sails (and a boom is a dangerous friend when working), much rowing was involved. Ignoring the safety aspect, few boats were decked or half-decked because the crews considered that in such boats the use of oars and the handling of lines was impeded. Reduced carrying capacity was another factor against decking. By the 1880s, boats of increasing length were becoming common, which also meant there were larger sizes of crews.

Hugh Miller of Cromarty, the author of *Letters on the Herring Fishing* and *Scenes and Legends of the North of Scotland*, who lost his father at sea, gives us a glimpse of life on these early nineteenth-century open boats:

> *The profession of fisherman is one of the most laborious
> and most exposed both to hardship and danger. From the
> commencement to the close of the fishing, the men who*

prosecute it only pass two nights of the week in bed. In all the others they sleep in open boats, with no other covering than the sail. In wet weather their hard couch proves peculiarly comfortless, and even in the most pleasant it is one upon which few besides themselves could repose.

Just over a century ago we could see Scottish boats evolving around two basic types. The Moray coast boasted of the 'Scaffie', an elegant, lug-sailed boat, manoeuverable but prone to problems in some weather conditions. Along the Fife coast and elsewhere the 'Fifie' evolved. Not so manoeuverable as the Scaffie, it took sail well. In 1879, following the marriage of a Lossiemouth man and the daughter of a 'Fifie' skipper, came the exciting birth, not of a baby fisherman, but of a boat. Called the 'Zulu' after the war taking place at the time, it possessed the best qualities of both boats and became the most famous lug-sailed fishing boat in Britain.

Steam appeared on the scene towards the end of last century. Initially it was seen as a supplementary source of power to the sail and for driving the winches. At first, funnels on the drifters were long and thin, positioned between the masts, and referred to as 'pipe stalkies'. As mechanical power took over from sail, the design of the drifters changed and with the later arrival of the paraffin engine, the features of the modern drifter became prominent; the single flush deck, the very upright superstructure, the bold shear of the prow and the straight stern.

Looking back over the years we can see that trawling was always more of an English tradition than a Scottish one. Those who did trawl had to put up with much antagonism because their activities were seen as detrimental to future stocks and jeopardising the livelihood of line fishermen. With trawlers being larger boats and more expensive to build, many fishermen became wage earners rather than self-employed. By 1903, nearly 300 steam trawlers had been built in Scotland and within thirty years, after diesel had taken over, their length would exceed 150 feet.

Fishing boats, until a score of years before the turn of the century, were made of wood. Steel took over from wood in the inter-war years when it was a cheaper commodity, but wood has frequently returned to the fore. The advantages of wood are many. Not being subject to corrosion, wood has a longer life. A wooden hull has greater natural buoyancy which gives better performance at sea. Being a poor conductor of heat (or cold) than steel, a wooden boat is warmer for the crew and requires less insulation to keep the hold cool; vibration is curtailed and there is less condensation. The fishing boat building business, it can only be said, faces a very uncertain future. Famous yards like Millers of St Monans with a history going back to 1747 and Hall and Russell of Aberdeen have closed down. Boat building skills will inevitably be lost. There is no doubt that fewer boats will be required in the future. Catching capacity is increasing and these boats will also have restricted time at sea for reasons of conservation. Shall we then see what has happened to our larger shipping industry repeated? Will tomorrow's fishing boats come off the stocks in Korea?

2
The Herring Trail

Circling uptide, the ring net surrounds the herring;
Both boats have their wheel-house lights to show
*   that they have shot,*
For the fleet is close now, shouting from deck to deck,
Robbie has shot, MacBride has shot, have a care man,
*   The net is easy torn.*

'The Alban Goes Out', Naomi Mitchison

Of all the saltwater heroes that adorn the pages of our literature, none is more intrepid or illustrious than Para Handy, skipper of the Clyde puffer, *Vital Spark*. And none are more knowledgeable and worldly wise. (We know because he has more or less told us so himself). So when Neil Munro's great character philosophises on the subject of herring, we do well to give him our full attention:

> *'Of aal the fish there iss in the sea,' said Para Handy,*
> *'nothing bates the herrin'; it's a providence they're*
> *plentiful and them so cheap! . . . The herrin' iss a great,*
> *great mystery. The more you will be catchin' of them*
> *the more there iss; and when they're no' in't at aal they're*
> *no there' – a great philosophical truth which the crew*
> *smoked over in silence for a few minutes.*

In his own way, Para Handy was pointing out that life has not always been kind to those who follow the herring. The giant shoals, for no apparent reason, are willing at times to forego their normally frequented areas. Records tell of herring disappearing from the Guilliam bank between Cromarty and Burghead for fifty years from 1730 and, after a short return, leaving again for another thirty years. Off the south of Sweden, they once returned to a location after an absence of seventy years. Legend, verse and song keep alive the great yesteryear catches of Loch Fyne and the River Forth. Man too, in addition to nature, has brought misery to Scottish herring communities. Great wars have savaged the export trade on which so many fisherfolk depended. Continentals, especially the Russians and the Germans, have long had a taste for herring. It is easy to forget that the loss of export trade brought about by the Russian Revolution brought misery to fishing communities far from that great land.

We think of the herring as a fish of the North Atlantic and the North Sea. Of the same family as the sprat and pilchard, it is a gregarious fish which feeds mainly on small crustaceans. The history of Scottish herring fishing can be traced back over many centuries with documents showing an early export trade to Holland. But, being a nation of seafarers, it was not long before the Dutch decided to fish Scottish waters themselves and by the Middle Ages theirs was the largest fleet fishing the North Sea. Having a distance to travel with their catches, it seems reasonable to give credence to the belief that the Dutch were the first to gut and salt herring while still at sea. Sir John Fastolf wrote himself into at least some of the English history books because of the Battle of the Herrings in 1629. When convoying supplies to the besiegers of Orleans, he formed a sort of laager of herring barrels and with his archers beat off the whole French army.

The Stuart kings made efforts to strengthen the home fishing fleet either by leglislation restricting foreign landings or by opening the coffers to support the building of fishing craft. The 1600s saw the Dutch introduce armed fishery protection but after their fleet was devastated by Admiral Duncan at the Battle of Camperdown, the Scottish herring fleet came into its own. Although it would be wrong to say a monopoly was achieved, there is no doubt that from then until the end of the nineteenth century the Scottish herring fleet held dominancy, with about three-quarters of the catch going for export after curing. The Shetland fish stations of Baltasound and Lerwick became supreme with landings equalling those of Aberdeen, Fraserburgh and Peterhead combined. In 1904, Lerwick and Baltasound landed over half a million crans. With a thousand herring to the cran, a simple calculation will show the economic importance of this sea harvest.

The migration and spawning habits of herring are unusual. Shoals approach our coast every summer to spawn and that is when fishing takes place. There is an apparent continuity to the migration pattern with the boats following the species and sub-species as they appear at different times round the coast. Indeed at one time it was thought the whole species took an annual migratory swim round the British Isles. June and July will see shoals off Wick, and by August, Peterhead and Aberdeen will be aware of their movement. Shoals will reach East Anglia by early autumn.

The west coast fishing stations too achieved fame. The great sea lochs like Fyne, Sunart and Broom enjoyed migrations. In the late 1700s three-hundred horses would be required every morning to carry the landings from the shore at Inverary. Seton Gordon in his *Highlands of Scotland* recounts:

> When the traveller Pennant visited Inveraray in 1771 some hundreds of boats each evening set their nets on Loch Fyne. On weekdays the cheerful noise of bagpipe and dance was heard by those on shore proceeding from the fishing fleet. On the Sabbath, each boat approaches the land, and Psalmody and devotion divide the day.

The Outer Hebrides also shared in the prosperity of the eighteenth century. The 1791 report, *Present State of the Scottish Fisheries* quotes:

*It was after the Union that the merchants of Stornoway
had full scope for their laudable pursuits; then it was, that
the herrings which they caught, might lawfully be sent to
the British West-India Islands, and exported thither, and
to all other lawful places, attended with the encouragement
of a bounty: from that time the people of Stornoway have
been steadily advancing. Now they can show in their
harbour, in the fishing time, upward of thirty sail of stout
handsome vessels, from twenty to seventy tons burden, all
their own property. Their town is a pattern of neatness
and cleanliness.*

In his own way Para Handy reminds us that over a century
later Loch Fyne was still the place for work and amusement:

*'The herrin' wass that thick in Loch Fyne in them days,'
recalled the Captain, 'that you sometimes couldna get
your anchor to the ground, and the quality was just sublime.
It wasna a tred at all so much as an amusement; you went
oot at night when the weans was in their beds, and you
had a couple o' crans on the road to Clyde in time for
Gleska's breakfast. The quays wass covered wi John O'
Brian's boxes, and man alive! but the wine and spirit
tred wass busy. Loch Fyne wass the place for life in them
days – high jeenks and big hauls; you werena very smert
if you werena into both o' them.'*

Para Handy was not wrong about the quality of Loch Fyne
herring. Dorothy Wordsworth visiting the area with her
brother noted in her 1803 *Diary*:

*Tuesday August 30th: Breakfasted before our departure,
and ate herring fresh from the water, at our landlord's
earnest recommendation – much superior to the herrings
we get in the north of England.*

Thanks to Lady Nairne and her song, 'Caller Herrin' we
remember the Forth was a prolific source of herring. In the
early 1800s a hundred boats could be seen fishing between
Bo'ness and the Fife coast. However, as the herring disappeared in quantity from many of our sea lochs and the

shoals had to be pursued further out to sea, a change in practice came about. Steam drifters arrived on the scene in the late 1800s carrying a hundred nets which could extend over two miles. The more prosperous east and north-east stations now took dominance over those in the west.

The herring lays its heavy and sticky spawn on rough, rocky sea-bed. Readily devoured by flatfish the spawn is especially appealing to haddock. As fry, the herring faces pursuit from conger, coalfish and lythe and increasing maturity brings it to the attention of gulls, cormorants and other sea birds. In the old classic documentary film, John Grierson's *The Drifters*, the trials of the herring are brought home. Trapped by the gills in a drift net, the herring are savaged by dogfish, delighted to find prey unable to escape their marauding.

But that documentary film, while exposing the cruelty of raw nature, also shows the remarkable staunchness and courage of fishermen. Standing for hour after hour on a heaving deck, in a biting cold, working with nets heavy with fish and moisture, short of sleep and far from home, facing the lottery of catch and market: how, one wonders, can such a life get into a man's blood? To quote D.T. Holmes:

> *The romance of the sea is apt to vanish as you look out upon a wilderness of foamy water, tossing the boat like an insignificant toy, drenching the bulwarks and vehemently smiting everything in its riotous anger. Neptune seems a mere blind force without reverence or mercy for the works of man.*

In the documentary too, one sees the smiling faces of the fish-gutters, those fisher lassies who followed the fleets from Shetland to East Anglia. Gutting sixty herring to the minute, fingers bandaged with cloots to limit knife-cuts and keep the salt farlin vat from adding to their pain, rain or cold seems unable to remove cheerfulness from their faces. Think as hard as you can, Have you ever seen a newspaper photograph or postcard of these fish-gutters where they did not have laughing faces? The Gaelic poet Derick S. Thomson gives us a photograph in words:

Their laughter like a sprinkling of salt
showered from their lips,
brine and pickle on their tongues,
and the stubby short fingers that could handle fish,
or lift a child gently, neatly, safely, wholesomely, unerringly,
and the eyes that were as deep as a calm.

The topsy-turvy of history had made them
slaves to short-arsed curers,
here and there in the lowlands, in England.
Salt the reward they won
from those thousands of barrels,
the sea-wind sharp on their skins,
and the burden of poverty in their kists,
and were it not for their laughter
you might think the harp-string broken.

'The Herring Girls'

The food value of herring is well known. The herring is more nourishing and contains more necessary vitamins and minerals than any other fish, flesh or fowl. It is a tragedy that so many people lost the taste, or did not have the opportunity to develop a taste for herring, when, because of lack of conservation measures and declining stocks, bans on fishing for herring had to be introduced in the late 1970s. The drastic action was effective and the early Eighties saw a slow but steady build-up to larger spawning stocks. But if the home consumer is not now showing the same enthusiasm for herring, the same cannot be said, as has been noted, for other peoples.

Herring are at their best in the summer and early autumn when they are full of feeding and plump in appearance. There is no close season but those caught in the spring are generally thin and tasteless. Being a 'fatty' fish, it cannot be cured by simple salting and drying or it would soon become rancid. Heavy salting and smoking over a wood fire is needed if it is to be transported far distances. And although no food needs less embellishment to grace a gourmet's plate than herring, in this age of cordon bleu cooks and sophisticated eating habits, curers and canners are evolving some highly acceptable variations on traditional themes; mustard and dill are two additives that readily spring to mind as special treats with herring. Kippered, rolled in oatmeal, soused – take your pick. The herring in one of its many forms, warrants our gastronomic affection and our respect.

3
Finnans and Smokies

I mind the time (and it's no far past)
When he wasna for fleein' alang sae fast,
An' doon i' the causey his cairt wad stand
As he roared oot 'Haddies!' below his hand;

'Pride', Violet Jacob

From Robert Fergusson to Violet Jacob, the haddock or 'haddie' figures in the poetry of our land. Perhaps it is little wonder. For poetry thrives on colour and charisma and the haddock has supplied these in abundance. The gold and brown of the finnan haddie and its slightly southern sister the Arbroath smokie seduces our palates through the eyes. The memory of blue-clad fishwives wielding their fish baskets remains strong with older generations. Craft shops and the like with their souvenir fishwife dolls and fishing artefacts will make sure a memory is not erased.

The haddock comes from the cod family with which it shares a barbule at the point of the lower jaw. Brown-backed and silver bellied it has a distinctive black spot behind each of its pectoral fins. Legend has it these spots are the finger and thumb marks of Saint Peter who took tribute money from the mouth of a haddock. This is one legend we should keep at a distance – haddock are not found in the Mediterranean, far less in the fresh water of Lake Gennesaret.

The haddock is a fish of the North Atlantic, found anywhere between Norway and Newfoundland. Its main spawning grounds are off Trondheim, south-west Iceland and the Faroes where it spawns between March and June. Getting most of its food near the bottom of the sea bed, it has a special liking for sand eels and herring spawn. Although still found in big shoals around our shores at particular times of the year, stocks are suffering from over-fishing. Haddock size and quality vary with location, the best fish coming in the main from deep water and the east coast, although Dublin Bay has hit the record books with a fish of sixteen pounds.

The 'haddie' is at its best between October and January whereas March and April see it at its worst. The haddock needs to be handled well and is generally gutted at sea, the skin being kept on to avoid tearing the soft flesh. It does not take salt as well as cod, one reason why so much haddock is cured by drying and smoking.

The Angus cliff-top village of Auchmithie is credited with originating the Arbroath smokie. A walk down the back streets of Arbroath near to the harbour will show to what extent the production of smokies is a true cottage industry. In my young days, it seemed as if every second house carried a notice indicating the activity being carried out in its back yard.

The fish to be smoked are tied in pairs, still with the skin on and suspended on a rod over a whisky barrel containing burning wood chips, sunk into the ground. Unlike the finnan haddie, the Arbroath smokie is ready to eat without further cooking after its smoking is complete. The skin is removed before re-heating (smokies are also delicious cold); a standby Dundee meal is to remove the flesh from the bones and mix and heat it with an egg, a meal that brings to mind the American Lady's Farewell:

How can I leave the marmalade
An' bonnets of Dundee?
The haar, the haddies and the brose,
The east wind blowing free!

'Penelope in Scotland', Kate Douglas Wiggin

21

A few miles south of Aberdeen lies the village of Findon. Findon's place in the culinary hall of fame is assured as here, certainly centuries ago, was developed the finnan haddock. The finnan's taste earned such wide appeal, it was perhaps inevitable that other ports landing haddock would jump on the bandwaggon and offer a similar cure with the result that a false and inferior product can now be found.

It is interesting that whereas Fergusson wrote about haddocks in, 'Caller Oysters' it is Finnans that get the mention in 'Leith Races':

> *The Buchan bodies, thro' the beach,*
> *Their bunch of Findrams cry:*
> *And skirl out bauld, in Norlan speech,*
> *'Guid speldins; – fa will buy?'*

Dean Ramsay when writing *Scottish Life and Character* a century later was obviously put out by the word 'Findrams' which he did not know. Wishing to educate his readers, or possibly concerned about his reputation and integrity, the good man thought it appropriate to include copious notes about the word:

> *Findon, or Finnan haddies, are split, smoked and partially*
> *dried haddocks. Fergusson, in using the word 'Findrams',*
> *which is not found in our glossaries, has been thought to be*
> *in error, but his accuracy has been verified, singularly*
> *enough, within the last few days, by a worthy octogenarian*
> *Newhaven fisherman, who remarked 'that it was a word*
> *commonly used in his youth: and above all', he added,*
> *'when Leith Races were held on the sands ye was like to*
> *be deeved wi' lang-tongued hizzies skirling out "Aell a*
> *Findram Speldrains?" and they jist ca'ed it that to get a*
> *better grip o't wi' their tongues.'*

Of course, these haddies might just have come from Fife? George Gourlay writing in the last century recalls:

> *It was an anecdote of the bookseller's shop in Anstruther*
> *shore that the 'Finnan Haddie' was so highly esteemed by*
> *the reigning sovereign – George IV – that the mail-coach as*

regularly as the letter-bag, carried a prime parcel from the little Banchory village for the royal breakfast. The waggish collector told a stupid joke that 'Letter Maggie' had been seen freighted from the post office with a mysterious packet, which was nothing less than a royal order to have the palace supplied from Anstruther . . .

Haddock for smoking must be plump and fresh, as stale fish will have a poor taste and the true creamy yellow colour will not be obtained. The head is always cut off before smoking, the fish opened to the vent and the skin brushed or scraped off. In complete contrast to the Arbroath smokie, the finnan is cut down the side of the backbone from neck to tail, the backbone normally lying on the left side. The split fish is then placed in a brine solution and this contributes to the shine or gloss of the finnan. Smoking then follows and the flesh darkens during the cooling period.

The haddock has always been a more revered fish in Scotland than in England. Indeed at one time English fishermen threw it back over the side to make way for species more attractive to the English palate. And it was only in the second half of the last century that smoking houses started to operate in Hull and Grimsby. Perhaps what is even more surprising is that English chefs have never developed an equivalent dish to Cullen Skink, the incomparable soup made from finnan haddies.

4
Other Sea Fish

Break, break, break,
On thy cold grey stones, O Sea!
And I would that my tongue could utter
The thoughts that arise in me.

'Break, Break, Break', Alfred Lord Tennyson

Cod

Fish cakes, fish fingers, fish pies: the cod has become our great manufacturing fish. Yet just as the haddock is seen as predominantly a Scottish taste, so one intuitively associates cod with other parts of the United Kingdom. Not that it doesn't present a fine sight lying full out in a fishmonger's window and not that the Scot is too proud to eat fish fingers; he and she eat a full share. But, appealing to our taste buds or not, it has failed to enter our folklore, achieve the status of a birthday treat, or excite the passion of the cordon bleu cook. The cod is seen in Scotland to have its rightful place in the fish finger.

Yet the cod has probably roused more passion, caused more international disputes and figured in more political harangues than any other fish. Disputes with Denmark and Iceland over cod fishing grounds can be traced back over many centuries; formal cod fishing treaties go back to 1490. Cod in these early days had a special importance. The Western world was a largely Catholic place with meat a forbidden food by Papal Decree on more than a quarter of the days of the year. Fish was an obvious alternative dish, but where was the necessary quantity to be found?

When Cabot returned from his voyage of discovery in 1497 with tales of fish swarming in such numbers near Newfoundland that they could be scooped out of the sea in a basket, to the French, Spanish and Basques it must have seemed like the discovery of El Dorado. For the next 400 years men would arrive in sailing ships to fish for cod on the 'Banks of Newfoundland' that area of underwater plateau where, to quote the Lüneburg Marine Museum Society, 'the unique mixture of cold Arctic and warm Southern waters, sunlight and seaborne nutrients supports a flourishing marine life'. Caught by handlines cast from the deck, the cod at that time were gutted and salted at sea by the European Continental fishermen before being stored in the hold and were brought home in a 'moist or green' condition. English boats, and later boats from Scotland, lacking cheap supplies of salt had to preserve their fish by drying them in the sun. Thus it was to safeguard fishing interests and provide havens for fishing fleets that the Maritime Provinces of Canada were initially settled.

Readers of Kipling's fine novel about fishing on 'the Banks', *Captains Courageous*, (later made into a film with Spencer Tracy in the lead role) may recall that by the mid-nineteenth century the handlining from schooners had been superseded by the use of dories. Dories were small, flat-bottomed two-man boats that could be stacked on deck, one inside the other, to save space. At the fishing grounds the dories were launched and their crews set trawl lines with their hundreds of hooks, on the ocean bottom. The dories then allowed the mother ship to cover much more ground and catches rose dramatically, benefiting not only the shipowners but the slave-owners of the West Indies who valued cod as a diet for their slaves. The work of a dory fisherman was hard. Launched in a small open boat, he was exposed to storm and cold, with the ever-present fear of being lost in the famous fogs of 'the Banks'. Kipling's descriptive pen makes us shiver as we read:

*For days they worked in a fog – Harvey at the bell – till,
grown familiar with the thick airs, he went out with Tom
Platt, his heart rather in his mouth. But the fog would not
lift, and the fish were biting, and no one can stay helplessly
afraid for six hours at a time. Harvey devoted himself to his
lines and the gaff or gob-stick as Tom Platt called for them;
and they rowed back to the schooner guided by the bell and
Tom's instinct, Manuel's conch sounding thin and faint
beside them. But it was an unearthly experience, and, for
the first time in a month, Harvey dreamed of the shifting,
smoking floors of water around the dory, the lines that
strayed away into nothing, and the air above that melted
on the sea below ten feet from his straining eyes.*

*. . . They made another berth through the fog, and that
time the hair of Harvey's head stood up when he went out
in Manuel's dory. A whiteness moved in the whiteness of
the fog with a breath like the breath of the grave, and there
was a roaring, a plunging and spouting. It was his first
introduction to the dread summer berg of the Banks, and he
cowered in the bottom of the boat while Manuel laughed.*

And the retrieving of the dories when a gale was blowing
was scarcely less of a danger:

*The boys stood by the dory-tackles with lanterns, the men
ready to haul, one eye cocked for the sweeping wave that
would make them drop everything and hold on for the dear
life. Out of the dark would come a yell of 'Dory, dory!' They
would hook up and haul in a drenched man and a half sunk
boat till their decks were littered down with nests of dories.
Five times in their watch did Harvey, with Dan, jump at the
fore-gaff where it lay lashed on the boom, and cling with
arms, legs, and teeth to rope and spar and sodden canvas as
a big wave filled the decks. One dory was smashed to pieces
and the sea pitched the man head first on to the decks,
cutting his forehead open: and about dawn, when the racing
seas glimmered white along their cold edges, another man,
blue and ghastly, crawled in with a broken hand, asking
news of his brother.*

'Captains Courageous'

26

With so much danger ever-present, it is not surprising that a religious way of life was commonplace. A retired Scots fisherman who had sailed out of Nova Scotia to the Banks in his young days, confirmed to the writer the behaviour of the Banks fishermen and told how for months at a time he would never hear a swear-word at sea. Perfection of course can never be achieved and there is the delightful story of a Newfoundland skipper who after his ship was tied up for the winter would spend his time drinking and carousing. When spring came round, he would make for the Salvation Army Citadel to seek salvation. Through the fishing season he was a model of piety and virtue, castigating ruthlessly any doryman heard uttering bad language. But, when his ship was laid up again for the winter, he would backslide from the Salvation Army and return to the binge. As spring again approached, it was a 'back to the Citadel' repeat performance. He knew that on the Banks, help was needed from every source.

While there is reason to believe Scots were fishing as far away as Iceland in the 1400s, their involvement in the Banks has, in the main, been as crew members serving other nationalities. Robert Burns though lets us know the giant Newfoundland dog was well-known in Scotland in his time and that Scottish fishermen were not strangers to the Banks. Do you remember his description of Caesar in 'The Twa Dogs'?

His hair, his size, his mouth, his lugs,
Shew'd he was none of Scotland's dogs,
But whalpet somewhere far abroad,
Where sailors gang tae fish for cod.

Our later folk songs too are rich in reference to cod fishing on the Banks; these can be found in Norman Buchan and Peter Hall's 'The Scottish Folk Singer'.

Last night as I lay on my bunk I dreamt a pleasant dream;
I dreamt I was back in Scotland beside a flowing stream.
The girl I loved sat on my knee and a bottle in my hand,
But I woke up broken hearted on the Banks of Newfoundland.

'Banks of Newfoundland', Trad.

The Banks no longer represent a seemingly inexhaustible source of cod. Climatic changes have reduced the feed for the species; over-fishing has taken its toll. Today Scottish fishermen look to the North Atlantic. But the story about a Shetland skipper known as 'Old Heglie' who, seeking shelter from a storm off south-west Iceland, discovered he had positioned himself over a bank which would that season give him a catch of 200,000 cod and become known as 'Heglie's Bank' is not likely to be repeated.

The cod is a demersal fish, a bottom feeder. Living on small fish, it prefers a rocky to a muddy sea bed and hunts by sense of smell, its eyesight being especially poor. Cod are mostly caught by trawling. While generally under three feet in length, fish over fifty pounds weight are not uncommon. The heaviest recorded cod weighed in at 211 pounds. The female fish lays millions of eggs – readily believed by the sight of those gloriously large roe poches lying on the fish-mongers' marble slabs.

Mackerel

How does a fish get a bad name? For years the poor mackerel was spoken about in derogatory terms: 'It's a scavenger fish, a dirty fish.' Well, the public has at last changed its mind, recognised that the mackerel's own eating habits are in line with those of other fish, and that mackerel products are worthy of a place on the delicatessen shelf. Smoked mackerel, mackerel paté, peppered mackerel, mackerel flakes and so on, are tasty party fare. Mackerel do suffer the disadvantage of tainting readily and losing flavour at speed. Mackerel's quick decomposition in hot weather was recognised by a London ordinance in the seventeenth and eighteenth centuries allowing them to be sold immediately before and after divine service on a Sunday.

Mackerel are one of the first fish to be caught by youngsters. A line with coloured feathers or glinting lures is sufficient to ensure sport when a shoal is about. For many years such line fishing was a common commercial

Dover Sole landed at the harbour, Dunbar 1890s.

Off to the fishing grounds — Peterhead.

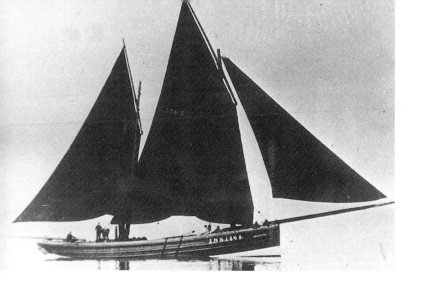

"Pansy" — a Zulu.

William Watson
and wife,
Skipper of the
"Fiery Cross".
Known as "Fiery
Cross" Watson
— Cellardyke.

Steam drifters — herring. Wick pre 1914.

Steam drifter — "Excelsior".

Herrings
(gutted)
for the
packers.

1934. Zulus, Fifies and Scaffies leave Anstruther.

Firth of Forth — hauling herring nets.

Harbour at Port Seton. Fishermen mending nets 1960s.

Pulling in drift net.

Doorstep
selling.

Tiny harbour,
Latheronwheel,
Caithness.

Klondiker.

1984 — Firth of Clyde Herring Pair — trawl comes alongside.

1985 — Skipness, Kintyre. Herring pair trawl. After hauling, the bag comes alongside and is taken forward for lifting.

method in dealing with the large shoals that swarm around Scotland in the summer and early autumn months, the west coast being more productive than the east. Seine-netting is now the most important method of catching mackerel by Scottish boats. This method of fishing has its dangers when seas are not at their kindest and consequently supplies to market can be erratic. While not all for home consumption, the Scottish mackerel landings which increased dramatically from 1,000 tons in 1970 to over 50,000 tons in 1977 are an indication of the increasing popularity of the fish. The eastern Europeans, especially the factory freezing ships of Poland, Bulgaria and Russia, being excluded from fishing EEC waters, are big buyers of mackerel. So much so that in recent years mackerel has come after haddock, cod and whiting in the league table of fishing earnings. Inevitably, stocks are declining.

The flat fish

> I feel the touch of a future
> In the cold. The little fish
> Come not near me, cleaving
> To their element and flattening on the sand.
>
> 'Tom on the Beach', George Bruce

The range of flat fish that grace the table and appeal to the palate is considerable. From the handsome halibut to the humble dab, devotees can be found. The more one studies flat fish, the more amazed one becomes at how perfectly they have adapted to their environment. Sea bottom feeders, the underbody bears little colouring while the exposed upper side carries colour expressing significant sympathy with the fish's environment. When young, flatfish, like other fish, are symmetrical with an eye on either side of the spine. But as they mature, they lose their symmetry and appear off-centre, more to one side of the spine than the other, and the 'flattening' process seems to owe more to a sideways pressure than a bashing from above. Frequently, one eye appears to have just scraped on to the top side of the fish because of good luck. Sandy bottoms where they can burrow into the sea bed are attractive habitats to flat fish. Spring sees the fish move towards the shore for spawning.

While a UK perspective might suggest the halibut as the king of the flat fish, Scottish ratings would not give it that position. Perhaps its high price has something to do with it. More likely it is because halibut is seldom at its best in Scottish fishmongers. Most halibut in the past have been landed from the deep water port of Hull and transport north has cost the fish its bloom. Signs of change are with us.

Following the splendid work done by the Sea Fish Industry Authority at Acharacle, the farming of halibut is now moving into an era where most production problems have been solved and the profit margin is conducive for fish farming development. The near future is likely to show halibut steaks featuring much more often on the menu. And such steaks they might be. If you have the time to wait, perhaps fifty years, halibut are capable of growing up to 500 pounds in weight – one reason why they are pursued by game fishermen seeking excitement. With some record specimens to its credit, the sea off Caithness has become a 'Mecca' for such activity in recent years.

The word 'sole' is said to be derived from the Latin, '*solea*' meaning a sandal (presumably describing its shape). This is probably the most popular flat fish in Scotland at the present time. Although it is found right around the Scottish coast, the North Sea, especially south of the Humber, provides the major fishing grounds. Sole is a dainty fish, normally caught in the half-pound to two-pound range. Its eyes are biased towards the right side of its body and it has a rounded head and small mouth. Lemon sole, at one time known as sand sole, differs from the common sole in having specks instead of blotches on its top side. Its much more oval shape makes it distinctly different from the common sole.

One wonders how it is that fish of the same shape, living in the same area under the same conditions and being sustained on the same food, can taste so different. Even blindfolded, it is difficult to confuse plaice with sole. Sole has a delicacy – the word respectability comes to mind – whereas plaice has a piquancy. Easily recognised by the orange and red spots on its brown upper side, plaice grows to a larger size than sole. But again, although caught around the entire coast, they are most prolific in the southern parts of the North Sea.

5
Shellfish

Lobsters

There was a stirring in the third fisherman's house.
The door opened very slowly. A thin face with huge
glinting eyes in it peered out. A long finger was
licked and held up to the sky. The head shook. 'No,'
said the scarf, 'not this morning'. 'I was out all
Saturday for one lobster and two crabs.'

'Greenvoe', George Mackay Brown

The lobster is undoubtedly king of the shellfish. Even lying on a marble slab in a fishmonger's window, its orange-red colour proclaims its regality. If marine creatures were to be accorded family mottoes, 'Wha dare meddle wi' me?' would be a fitting label for this armoured-plated and well-armed crustacean.

The lobster is a creature of the sea bed where it feeds on live or dead fish and other shellfish. Although capable of growing to over ten pounds in weight, most caught lobsters are in the one to three pound range. Their claws, which differ in shape, contain much prized flesh. The left or crusher claw is thicker and heavier than the righ or ripper claw with its many small teeth. Most of the lobster's white flesh is in the tail which can be flapped downwards so allowing it to swim backwards when such a tactical move is expedient. The males and females are distinct, the female visibly carrying her eggs or berries on swimmerets under her tail. Its pugnacious nature sees the lobster in many a scrape where it may lose a limb. But its powers of regeneration are considerable, replacement claws and legs growing again although several moults are necessary before the new member reaches the size of the original.

Lobsters increase in size by casting their outer shell and growing a larger one. This may happen once or twice a year when the lobster puffs itself out with water to fill the larger shell until new body growth fills the carcass.

Lobsters in their natural state are a purple-blue colour, the change to red being brought about by boiling. Provided the water is absolutely boiling, immersion is the most practical way of killing a lobster. The pot or pan used for this purpose must be well filled with boiling water so that immersion is not followed by a drop in temperature. A two per cent salt solution should be used and boiling time ranges from twenty to thirty minutes depending on size. The meat should not be picked until the cooling is completed. There are some who contend the best way to dispatch a lobster is by putting a knife into the junction of hard shell and tail and cutting towards the head and tail. But if you don't have a surgical leaning, stick to immersion.

Scottish lobsters are of a superb quality. Because of the worldwide demand for them, most lobsters are destined for foreign parts, frequently being flown in the live state in tanks. Abroad they command higher prices than the home market would tolerate. Regretfully the sight of sea-side shops selling modestly priced lobster sandwiches as one comes across in North America (not to mention 'surf on turf', lobster on a steak) is found only in Brigadoon in Scotland.

Because they are such a luxury dish in Scotland many chefs give them a treatment which warrants the diner having a sleeping-off period. Do you remember the last verse of the poem by Robert Service about the man who went swimming after doing justice to a large lobster for lunch?

But George, alas! came never back.
Of him they failed to find a trace;
His wife and kids are wearing black,
And miss a lot his jolly face . . .
But oh how all the lobsters laugh,
And write in wrack his epitaph.

'Lobster for Lunch'

Being a high priced food with demand exceeding supply, thoughts have inevitably turned to increasing the supply of lobsters by farming. Unfortunately, while the rearing of lobsters under controlled conditions is perfectly feasible, the economics are not attractive. The main reason for this is that the lobster, right from the beginning is a most unfriendly beast: he is a cannibal; warfare is his hobby. This means that rearing has to be done on an individual pen basis and the provision for such housing for four or five years, plus the time required to reach a good table weight, is not a monetary proposition. Other ways of increasing the population are being tried. The approach presently being tried by the Sea Fish Industry Authority and other research bodies is to release hatchery reared lobsters at between two and four months of age onto selected areas of sea bed where their possibilities for growth are good. The success of this approach will not be known for some time yet.

Meantime, when exercise is needed, try dancing the 'Lobster Quadrille'. For how to do it, read *Alice in Wonderland*.

Crabs

Is this the time to spin a thread,
When Colin's at the door?
Rax down my cloak – I'll to the quay,
And see him come ashore.

'The Sailor's Wife', William Julius Mickle

For many years the cheery-faced crab was considered an almost worthless object. It has struggled over the years to come into its own. Writing over a century ago, George Gourlay acknowledged the debt owed by Fife fishers to the newly introduced railway for developing a market:

> *Any day they [crabs] were to be gathered in bushels*
> *amongst the low water rocks, no one thinking them worth a*
> *king's coin, unless, perhaps, when a 'twapenny' or two was*
> *given to a needy neighbour for saving you trouble about a*
> *little parcel for an old friend in the city, who still retained a*
> *schoolboy liking for 'wilks and partan taes'. Old John*
> *Robertson, of the herring kiln, tried to storm the Dundee*
> *palate with crabs so far preserved by the boiling process, but*
> *in the end he had to confess, 'they didna pay kindling for the*
> *big pat'. Till the iron horse was put into harness the partan*
> *was of so little value that a 'dizen o big taes for a penny'*
> *was an everyday errand to the fisher's door. Now however,*
> *a new industry has been added to the coast, and with the*
> *miners and cotton spinners of Lancashire, not to speak of*
> *Billingsgate amongst the customers, the price of this once*
> *despised shell fish has become fourfold in twenty years.*

Many would declare the crab is still undervalued and it is difficult to be sure why the crab has never attained the cachet of the lobster. Many a fisherman with ready access to both has declared his preference for crab meat. Possibly the readiness to maximise profits by mixing the two colours of flesh in the crab has something to do with it. Perhaps it has an unfortunate image as being suitable only for duty as a paste. But the growing demand for crab-meat from the Continent will ensure it moves steadily up-market.

Caught in creels like lobster, the crab has a squat body. The male, carrying larger claws and more meat than the female, has greater market value. Like the lobster it has powers of regeneration and casts it shell in the growth process. The female carries its eggs attached to its legs. An interesting difference between the edible crab and the common shore crab so often seen on beach and rock, is that the former, when lifted up, tucks its claws and legs underneath its body while the shore crab spreads these appendages out.

Crabs do not store or travel well and processing near to where they are landed is common practice. Crabs must be killed before boiling otherwise they will shed their limbs when being boiled. Killing is done either by 'drowning' in fresh water or by spiking through the nerve centre located at the vent and just above the mouth. Crabs must always be well cooked otherwise potentially dangerous bacteria may not be killed.

Recent years have seen Continental buyers develop markets for crabs apart from the well known so-called edible crab. Interest from Spain has centred on the velvet crab, a swimmer which, like the lobster, turns red when cooked.

Mussels

> At Musselburgh, and eke Newhaven,
> These fisher-wives will get top livin',
> When lads gang out on Sunday's even
> To treat their joes,
> And tak of fat pandours a prieven,
> Or mussel brose.
>
>   'Caller Oysters', Robert Fergusson

The common sea mussel can be found right around the Scottish coast. It is especially abundant in clean conditions where salt and fresh water meet such as the mouths of burns entering sea lochs. The Firths of Forth and Tay, Cromarty and Dornoch, the Ythan estuary and the reaches of Clyde and Solway can all boast a past, if not a present, of large productive mussel beds.

A sedentary creature, the mussel possesses an anchoring system. It secretes strong threads which attach to hard ground allowing itself the ability to move upwards by extending the range of this byssal thread. Spawning mainly occurs during the winter months, fertilisation taking place in the sea. The offspring larvae swim freely for some weeks before attaching themselves to suitable anchorages from where they will grow to maturity. Mussels which live below the low water mark and so are always covered by the sea, grow more quickly than those exposed by the movement of the tide. The quantity and succulence of the flesh varies throughout the year being at its best in the run up to spawning in the autumn and early winter.

Fergusson's reference to mussel brose is one of the few about mussels in Scottish poetry. It is surprising that it is in the context of food. While the English have long eaten mussels, it has little history as a favourite meal in Scotland. The enormous beds of mussels found around Scotland last century were destined, not for the stomachs of the rich or poor but for the bait lines. Mussel was the prime bait on lines and, with a hook every two feet for miles and miles of line, the harvesting of mussels for bait was a harsh chore for the individual fisherman and his family, and a sizeable feeder industry for the boats. In the 1890s, at Collieston in Aberdeenshire, the wives of fishermen walked three miles to the mussel beds with creels on their backs and after wading far out into the cold Ythan estuary to collect their bait, carried their loads the three miles back to their village. Angus Martin of Campbeltown, who writes with authority on the fishing scene, describes the suffering of those youngsters obliged to work while chilled to the bone:

> He broke the ice and kicked at darkness.
> His basket tipped on its side
> and rocked on the bare ebb stones.
> Soon he would pack it up with mussels,
> with frozen hands unfastening them,
> a child's tears filming his eyes,
> that fisherman's son, torn from sleep,
> as a living fish, in its shell of grace,
> is riven from water.
>
> 'Bait Gathering'

Where the gathering of mussels had to be an operation of scale it was customary to use a dredge to which a strong net was attached and this was pulled by a small fishing boat. The way they operated dredges was not selective and immature stock found its way into the net along with the best bait. It is said that over 100,000 tons of mussels were lifted from the Clyde estuary last century. Eyemouth fishermen were known to have used over 900 tons in one year. Tom McGowran in *Newhaven – Port of Grace* tells of thirty boats from Peterhead and other places queuing up in the Forth to load mussels with some boats having to wait three weeks for a load. A harder attitude prevailed at Musselburgh where the local fishermen would only dispose of their surplus mussels to fishermen from other communities who were willing to sell their fish to Musselburgh fishwives for their Edinburgh trade, a neat way of restricting door-step competition.

Today Musselburgh makes sure its past importance in the fishing world is not forgotten with its 'Fishermen's Walk' held at the beginning of September. This walk is bound up in memory with the end of the summer fishing season and the gathering of money for the old and the poor. Local poet Wattie Livingstone has described the scene:

> They stretch back in their hunders, frae Bush Street past
>   the Wynd,
> The dark-blue Guernseyed fishermen, wi' their women-folk
>   behind:
> White hankies all a flutter, and striped petticoats,
> An' shawls o' Paisley pattern – while the band plays
> 'Weel Rows the Boat'.

> 'The Walk Day'

The Forth in general, of course, is much associated with the gathering of shellfish. Sir Archibald Geikie in his 'Scottish Reminiscences' shows that the area produced its quota of characters:

> On the South side of the Forth the fishwives of Newhaven, Fisherrow and Musselburgh have long been famous for their conservatism in the matter of the picturesque costume which they wear. Dunbar, once a busy port, and the centre of an important herring fishery, used to boast a number of queer oddities amongst its seafaring population. One of these men would now and then indulge in a prolonged carouse at the public house. After perhaps a day or two thus spent, he would return to his home, and, standing at the door, would take off one of his large fisherman's boots which he would

*pitch into the house, with the exclamation, 'Peace or war,
Meg?' If the goodwife still 'nursed her wrath to keep it
warm,' she would summarily eject the boot into the street.
Whereupon the husband, knowing that this was Meg's
signal of war, returned to his cronies. If, on the contrary,
the boot was allowed to remain, he might hope for
forgiveness, and crept quietly into the house.*

Sometimes the demand for mussels led to considerable
friction. In her history of the Cromarty Firth, Marinell Ash
tells how the Earl of Cromarty who held Barony rights to
the mussel beds at Nigg, had to defend the beds from
poachers from Buckie. At least the noble earl seems to have
attempted to maintain the stocks. The position of a later
guardian of the beds is not so clear. The Cromarty fishers
considered they had a right to take mussels from the beds
and this was disputed by the Duchess of Sutherland of the
time who took court action. The fishers won their claim, it
being noted that although oysters were mentioned in the
Barony charter, no reference was made to mussels. An
unwillingness to restock led to the inevitable – the beds
were depleted by the end of last century.

The mussel is making a substantial appearance on the
Scottish table. Mussels have become an accepted starter for
a meal and they have also become a standard supermarket
line. And, one is glad to say, the brand names are not all
foreign.

While Holland, France and Spain have a long history of
mussel farming, such formal attempts in Scotland have
been mostly confined to reducing overcrowding in beds
and to simple transplanting to more suitable locations.
This, of course, is a logical and sensible way of farming
mussels, but not the best method to obtain the consistent
high-quality article the market demands. It was not until
the Aberdeen Marine Laboratory started west coast trials
in the late 1960s that the full potential for growing mussels
as a crop seems to have been realised. Using the Spanish
method of attaching parent stock to coarse-fibre ropes
suspended from rafts, trials carried out in Loch Sween,

chosen for its limited tide range and equable temperature, were extremely successful. Further work carried out by the Sea Fish Industry Authority has led the way for commercial development and a splendid home-produced article is now available. The rope production method scores over the working of beds, because the mussels are suspended in mid-water where the maximum amount of food is available. High meat yields are obtained, and, the mussels being off the ground, they do not become contaminated with grit and 'pearls'. While competition from the Far East, where a warmer climate encourages quicker growth and the producer, at present anyway, enjoys lower labour costs, will continue to be severe, the more temperate climate of Scotland provides a tastier mussel and one must feel optimistic about the future.

Kings and Queens

Limpets live in houses
which are portable,
but they never carry them far –
a foot and a bit, perhaps,
in any direction, grazing
the rock which is their sole domain,
a tenure unto death.

'Limpets', Angus Martin

The term 'clam' is widely used in Scotland to include the large 'king' scallop and its much smaller near relative, the 'queen' scallop. Why the latter should have figured so little in Scottish fare is something of a mystery. Indeed, for years, the queen was considered solely for bait purposes. That a counterpart to the New Englanders' vast consumption of Clam Chowder could be developed on this side of the Atlantic never seems to have been considered either by canners or others engaged in the marketing of produce from the sea. Perhaps the Scot just does not take to fish soups; even the worthy Cullen Skink is undervalued.

But there are abundant signs that scallops, and queens in

particular, are at last gaining their rightful place in the home market. Few dishes are more nutritious or more easily prepared. With a flavour more akin to lobster than prawn or crab, served in their fan-shaped shells, they add a certain something to the table.

The first scallop fishing was Clyde estuary and west coast based. Once very prolific, the Ayrshire and Stranraer beds have been heavily fished and boats now make for beds around many of the islands such as Jura, Mull and Skye. Orkney and Shetland produce some very high quality shells.

Scallop fishing was long seen as a winter occupation. There were good reasons for this. A limited home market meant that much of the catch had to be sent to London's Billingsgate Market for disposal and a long rail journey with stock which had to be kept alive was something to be avoided in warm weather if at all possible. Clams, being Spring spawners, are also at their best (with large roes) as that time of the year approaches. A fickle public considered that was the end of the season for them, however there has now been a realisation that scallops recover from spawning by early summer and that a year-round demand exists in the export trade if not at home. Consequently, almost year-round fishing has now become accepted practice.

Both king and queen scallops are found on sandy and muddy sea bottoms in a wide range of depths, even down to twenty-five fathoms or so. The king, unlike the more active queen, frequently recesses itself into the sea bottom. Skin-diving for scallops has recently come to the fore. While such a form of harvesting means a selection of good-sized shells, it is not conducive to a low cost on the slab. Most scallops are collected using a dredge which is towed along the sea floor. A toothed dredge which digs out the scallops lying in a recessed position is much favoured.

Scallop shells are irresistible to many people walking along a beach. The age of a scallop can be calculated much in the same way as that of a tree, the shell showing a concentric ring for every year of its life.

If the marketing of products derived from clams gathered in Scottish waters is not apparently extensive, one ventures to suggest that the position is changing. The hordes of holiday-makers making for the Atlantic seaboard resorts in the States are returning with a taste for Clam Chowder, the magnificent creamy soup with a reputation there akin to Scots Broth at home. At least one English soup manufacturer has seen the potential for this line and it figures on some supermarket shelves. Far Eastern countries, claiming unpolluted waters, are providing home canners with clams which, if not equalling the home product in size and quality, are nevertheless inexpensive and capable of attractive presentation. (One wonders if the East Indian giant clam with its hundredweight shell will reach our tables.) But what is being done to step up home production?

There has in fact been a remarkable increase in scallop farming over recent years because of pioneering work done by the Sea Fish Industry Authority and other bodies. Japanese methods in particular have been copied. Suspended lines or nets shaped like Japanese lanterns are the most popular approaches adopted. Live scallops though, still seem to be too expensive to be a regular buy. It is to be hoped that increasing production will see this most delectable food become as affordable as the gentle prawn has become. And a realisation that only the most modest amount of cooking is appropriate would not go amiss.

Prawns

It is not storm or calm, but yesterday
The wild winds leapt in sudden thunder down;
Shook the dark waters into starry spray,
And thrilled the soul of many a seaside town.

'The Sorrow of the Sea', John Hogben

The terms 'prawns' and 'shrimps' are often used to describe the same species. Diners do not worry themselves over-much with terminology. The man enjoying his potted shrimps does not enquire if he is eating brown shrimps or pink shrimps. The lady tucking into scampi assumes she is eating prawns. Let us not confuse her by suggesting she is eating Norway lobster from Dublin Bay. Let us keep life simple. The one distinction the shopper should make is between imported shrimps from the Far East and the meatier and more attractive looking North Atlantic prawn, 'Nephros Norvegicus'.

There was little public taste for prawns until around 1950 when a trade developed in Lossiemouth and Eyemouth. Looking back, it seems ludicrous to think that until that time, prawns taken in the trawl or seine-net were considered rubbish and returned to the sea, unless, of course, a member of the crew had developed a taste for them. By the mid-Fifties specialist gear had been introduced and in the next decade, changes in leglislation allowed trawling to replace seine-netting in the Moray, Forth and Clyde Firths. This provided the impetus for the prawn to become Scotland's most important shellfish species and it has become an income provider of special importance in the west and north-west inshore grounds as well as in the firths already indicated. Stocks have held up for many years with the Forth becoming the first area to display obvious signs of declining stocks.

Looking much like a small lobster, the prawn is a burrowing creature, foraging actively for food within the sea-floor mud. Like the lobster it moults regularly and can regenerate a lost limb. Maturity comes to the male prawn after three years when a size of around 85 mm is reached; females mature slightly earlier with a smaller size.

Once outside its burrow, the prawn falls prey to a number of predators, cod being its chief enemy. Work done at the Marine Laboratory in Aberdeen suggests there is a relationship between burrow emergence and light intensity; in other words, the more light reaching the sea bottom, the more likely prawns will be out of their burrows feeding. Certainly fishermen see a catch relationship between depth of water and time of day. Bad weather which of course inhibits the amount of light reaching the sea bottom seems to restrict catches.

As lovers of prawns will know, there are considerable fluctuations in their 'tastiness'. Much depends on their treatment after being caught. The sooner prawns can be eaten after leaving the sea the better. Just caught and boiled are best, but the bulk of the North Atlantic prawns we consume have either been quick frozen or kept in ice before cooking and much depends, in the latter case, on how long it takes the catch to reach the factory. Thawing out of frozen prawns in the home is of special importance. This must be done slowly if full flavour is to be enjoyed and too often people forget to use their refrigerator when thawing out. We have not yet developed the trade in this country that is common in the Far East for farmed river prawns, nor are the frozen raw headless prawns, so favoured by the Americans, widely available to us.

Oysters

At nicht round the ingle sae canty are we,
The oyster lass brings her treat frae the sea;
Wi' music and sang as time passes by,
We hear in the distance the creel lassies cry.
Caller o' u, Caller o'.

'Caller o' u', John Gray

'I suppose', wrote the eminent Professor Huxley many years ago, 'that when the sapid and slippery morsel – which is and is gone like a flash of gustatory summer lightning – glides along the palate, few people imagine they are swallowing a piece of machinery (and going machinery too) greatly more complicated than a watch – in fact a living organism of a high order.'

The great man spoke the truth. While everyone knows oysters are consumed alive, or at least half alive, few wish to think about the technicalities of valves, heart, kidney, labial palps and other bits and pieces that go to make up this delectable seafood.

Oysters live gregariously in beds normally at depths of over three fathoms. Fastidious as to location, they feed on minute organisms washed into the mouth. Because they lie in deep water, harvesting traditionally resulted in dredging, a non-selective method of procurement which meant the ultimate destruction of the immature molluscs. In earlier times, oysters were credited with intelligence because, being creatures without eyes or ears, they are clever enough to keep their shells shut in a retiring tide or when being handled or transported.

The accumulation of oyster shells in kitchen middens shows that man has long had pleasure from the oyster. It is known the Romans were appreciative of their taste and flavour. In Scotland, where they have not always been the prerogative of the well-heeled, we associate the oyster particularly with the east coast. The large natural west coast beds that existed, such as West Loch Tarbert, have long since disappeared. Edinburgh literature makes much of the oyster. In *Traditions of Edinburgh*, William Chambers gives some delightful descriptions of the oyster's contribution to eighteenth-century social life:

> . . . *the custom which prevailed among ladies, as well as gentlemen, of resorting to what were called oyster cellars, is in itself a striking indication of the state of manners during the last century. In winter, when the evening had set in, a party of the most fashionable people in town, would ajourn in carriages to one of those abysses of darkness and comfort, called, in Edinburgh, laigh shops, where they proceeded to regale themselves with raw oysters and porter, in a dingy room, lighted by callow candles. The rudeness of the feast, and the vulgarity of the circumstances under which it took place, seem to have given a zest to its enjoyment, with which more refined banquets could not have been accompanied. One of the chief features of an oyster-cellar entertainment was, that full scope was given to the conversational powers of the company. Both ladies and gentlemen indulged, without restraint, in sallies the merriest and the wittiest; which elsewhere would have been suppressed as improper, were here sanctified by the oddity of the scene, and appreciated by the most dignified and refined.*

And the poet Fergusson in his, 'Caller Oysters' makes reference to one of the most famous establishments for the holding of an oyster party:

> *When big as burns the gutters rin,*
> *If ye ha'e catched a droukit skin,*
> *To Luckie Middlemist's loup in*
> *And sit fu' snug,*
> *Owre oysters and a dram o' gin,*
> *or haddock lug.*

Thanks to the existence of many old records we know much about the Forth oyster trade. Before the eighteenth century was out, boats were regularly taking 4–5,000 oysters in a sweep and the total export trade from the Forth was in the region of 30 million oysters a year. The beds stretched solidly across the Forth from South Queensferry to Aberdour and down the south side of the river as far as Leith and Prestonpans. Further productive beds were found round the island of Inchkeith. The right to fish these oyster beds or scalps was given by Royal Charter, either to Burghs or individuals or to a Fishermen's Society. The boundaries though were in many cases not too tidily defined and disputes between the various interested bodies were frequent – not always resolved by recourse to the courts. Many battles took place at sea, sometimes involving more than twenty boats. Yet the vindictiveness felt does not appear to have been intense. Any 'prisoners' taken were usually given a meal before being sent home. The last big battle between warring bodies was in 1856.

The Forth oyster beds would have had a longer life had it not been for the introduction of the steam dredger which was capable of doubling the day's harvest achieved by rowing or sailing. The steam dredger also lifted more immature stock which naturally was worth less money. And as the merchants paid less, so the production of quality oysters in England by means of cultivated beds increased. Prices fell further, more dredging led to gluts. Increasing river pollution took its toll of the nursery stocks. The writing was on the wall.

Superstitions and the sea have long been bedfellows. Sailors, as the nautical will know, were in the habit of 'whistling up the wind' at times of calm when wind was needed to fill the sails. A look through old manuscripts suggests that singing was required to catch oysters. People on shore would regularly hear the music of songs carried over the water from oyster boats. Herd's *Ancient and Modern Scots Songs* of 1769 contains a 'Dreg Song' with the words:

> *The oysters are a gentle kin,*
> *They winna tak unless you sing.*
> *Come buy my oysters aff the bing,*
> *To serve the Sheriff and the king,*
> *And the commons o' the land,*
> *And the commons o' the sea.*

Sir Walter Scott in *The Antiquary* follows a similar suggestion:

> *The herring loves the moonlight,*
> *The mackerel loves the wind:*
> *But the oyster loves the dredging-sang,*
> *For they come of a gentle kind.*

Francis Collinson though in his study of the *Oyster Dredging Songs of the Forth,* brings us back to reality. He points out the songs were not sung for superstitious courtship reasons but to enable the rowers to maintain a steady rowing stroke. The dredge being towed behind the boat, had to have its bar going into the oyster beds at a forty-five degree angle. An increase in speed would lift the dredge off the sea floor, so missing the oysters; a decrease in speed would hinder the dredging. The interesting point is that most of the songs were impromptu, made up as the fishermen went along, a leader singing a line that offered itself, the crew repeating it in chorus. And like the singing of sea shanties, the lines could be nonsensical or robust, the actual words not likely to be heard on shore. *The Statistical Account of 1845*, referring to Prestonpans, considered the singing of dredging songs worthy of a mention:

> *. . .long before dawn, in the bleakest season of the year,*

*their dredging song may be heard from afar off, and, except
when the wind is very turbulent, their music, which is not
disagreeable, appears to be an accompaniment of labours
that are by no means unsuccessful.*

Today, there is a market for cheaply priced oysters; a
holiday in the Vendée will show that. Oyster-culture is no
novelty and most oysters eaten today are farmed products.
The French with their massive oyster beds running from
Biscay to Brittany, have shown what can be done under
today's conditions and with today's problems. Must we be
left behind?

An oyster in prime condition may be recognised by the
thin china tenuity of its shell with an opalescent lustre on the
inside. The flesh should be white and firm. With such a dish
on the table, one should be able to sing with John Rydon:

Let us roister with the oyster,
In the shorter days and moister
That are brought by brown September
With its roguish final 'R',
For breakfast or for supper
On the under shell or upper
Of dishes he's the daisy
And of shellfish he's the star.

'Oysters With Love'

6
Lines, Nets and Trawls

To caulk her oft can do none ill,
And tallow where the flood-mark flows;
Bot gif she leaks get men of skill
To stop her holes laich in the howes.

'The Fleming Barge', Robert Semphill

Those who study such things contend that spearing was the first instrument method of catching fish. Although the river spearing of salmon which continued into late last century is well documented, Scottish literature is sparse in its reference to the spearing of sea fish although archeologists sifting through middens of ancient settlements have frequently found harpoon-type bone tips in company with bone fish hooks. What is certain, is that the catching of fish by means of lines carrying baited hooks has existed since time immemorial. The principle has not varied over the centuries, only the materials and the scale of operation have changed.

Line-caught fish command a premium. Not suffering the rough treatment of trawl-caught fish their appearance and keeping qualities are enhanced. But this century has seen the near demise of such fishing because of its high-cost nature. And we find it difficult to come to terms with the harshness of the work, for both fishermen and their wives, that such fishing entails.

Line fishing is carried out either by small-lines or the larger scale long-lines. To the lines are attached dropper lines or snoods which carry a number of baited hooks. The coiling and storage of these lines on the boat is an art in itself as the lines may be many miles in length and may be carrying thousands of hooks. Thus the importance of a supply of mussels for bait and the need for a dedicated wife to bait the hooks. Most line fishing has been carried out for cod and haddock and it has the advantage that rough ground, unsuitable for trawling because of the damage it can do to the net, can be covered. Hauling in, especially before the introduction of motor line-haulers, was hard work and frequently much of the catch was savaged by other fish unable to resist the offer of an easy meal.

The net of course is the fisherman's main piece of equipment and its origins go back to well before biblical times. Stone Age remnants have been found in Egypt; also, paintings on monuments in Greece show nets in use. The Chinese at one time made nets from the cocoons of the wild silkworm, soaking them in an oil which made them barely visible in water.

To those brought up in fishing towns and villages with strong memories of the drunken movements of the drifters as they crossed the bar, that surging meeting-place of river and sea, the drift-net is well known. Drift-net fishing is carried out for those fish like herring and mackerel which congregate on or near the surface. A drift-net is suspended from floats and hangs like a curtain about two fathoms below the surface. It may be two miles or more in length and fish swimming into it are caught by the gills. Once the net has been shot, the boat is turned head-on into the wind to drift with the tide. (In the days of sail, the mizzen mast would be set to help keep the boat in this position.) After a few hours the net is hauled on board and the catch, if catch there be, is emptied into the hold.

It takes little imagination to appreciate the difficult decision facing a skipper when, with his drift-net out, the wind starts to blow. Hauling a heavy catch on board can take many hours and does nothing to add to the stability of the boat. Frequently the answer is to ride out the bad weather allowing the net to act as a sea anchor – not a pleasant experience. Yet bad as that picture is, try to imagine what it must have been like before the age of mechanisation. The hardship of pursuing shoals in an undecked boat by means of oar or sail, completely exposed to all the elements, soaked through with hand hauling in an age when oilskins had not been invented, is too much for our civilised minds to grasp. To quote W.S. Graham:

We are at the hauling then hoping for it
The hard slow haul of a net white with herring
Meshed hard.

'The Nightfishing'

Drift-nets suffer from hard usage and need regular mending. Before synthetic materials were used, the barking or tanning of nets was a weekly event. Saturdays traditionally saw the nets being immersed in great boiling vats of a tar solution which acted as a salt-water preservative. The nets were then laid out on the shore to dry before being stowed on deck for the next week's fishing.

Our mental picture of the sea-fishing scene is probably dominated by the drifter. To the landsman it expresses the romance of the sea. But other methods of catching fish have come into prominence. The origins of seine-netting are not known to us, but the logic of the method encourages us to believe it was within the compass of primitive man to explore. Captain Cook recorded South Sea fishermen using 'a long net like a seine' during his 1777 voyage and its use was known and developed in Loch Fyne around the middle of last century. The Scandinavians have long been users of the seine-net but its large-scale use by Scottish fishermen does not seem to have started until the 1920s when it became popular on the Moray Firth.

Seine-netting, or ring-netting as it has come to be called in some quarters, involves the sweeping of an area in a circular direction, where fish are believed to be present, from a fixed point, and back to that point, when the net is hauled. Originally, after the boat had concluded its sweep, the net would be hauled on to a beach. But net damage and the physical effort required for the operation, encouraged the move to hauling on board which led naturally to the need for larger and more sophisticated craft. The seine itself is a single continuous net, often likened to a purse, sometimes bigger than a football pitch, with a floating line on the top of the net and a weighted line at the bottom to ensure the net hangs down. The net is deeper in the middle than at the sides, to which long ropes are attached. On arrival at a fishing ground, an anchor and buoy, with one of the side lines attached are put overboard and the boat pays out the rope as it sets out on its sweep. After the net has been shot, the boat completes its circular sweep returning to the buoy; when the ropes attached to the net are winched in, the net forms a kind of large purse as this operation is completed. A rough sea bottom plays havoc with a seine-net, and areas free from obstacles like the Moray Firth and the seas around the Bell Rock are favoured for this method of fishing. The paying out of line and the sweep is a fairly quick operation and is repeated many times during the day. Haddock and plaice are the most common fish caught in Scotland by seine-netting. More recently, mid-water netting has come to the fore, an operation involving two boats working together.

Trawlers are the big business end of the fishing world, accounting for well over half of the fish landed. Aberdeen is the major Scottish trawler port, the boats seeking their catches as far away as Iceland. The trawl seeks out the bottom feeding fish, not only cod and haddock, whiting, pollack and ling, but the whole range of flat fish from sole to skate and halibut.

The trawl net, which may be more than fifty yards in length, is dragged along the bed of the sea. The trawlhead includes a 'tickling' arrangement which stirs the ground, encouraging those fish which like to lie partially buried to rise into the net. The tail (or 'cod end' as it is called) of the net is capable of being loosened so that the catch when brought on board can be easily emptied out. A certain amount of agility is required during emptying to avoid being smothered by the catch.

Although many a crab finds its way into the trawl net, the common method of catching the edible crab and the more up-market lobster, is by use of creels. Creels are no more than cages that the crabs and lobsters are enticed to enter under the promise of food, and from which exit is difficult. Although only made of a net-covered framework, the handling of creels is surprisingly hard work. Weighted to remain on the bottom, the weight, added to the wooden frame which ultimately becomes sodden, combines to give a hefty load when being removed from the sea for re-baiting or emptying, especially when the creels are joined together in a line. Although a creel may catch both crabs and lobsters, where crabs are the main catch a larger eye for entry is usually given; fresh bait, it is argued by some fishermen, is preferable to old although the proof of this is sketchy. To meet their more destructive nature, less netting and more wood are used in the construction of the creels.

The first nets were made by hand but by the early 1800s James Paterson of Musselburgh had invented his net-loom which was subsequently improved upon by Walter Ritchie from the same town. The earliest nets were made from hemp and cotton and various treatments such as tarring had to be given to reduce the adverse effects of sea water on the netting. The introduction of synthetic materials for nets while improving their longevity, has led to the collapse of a significant local commercial infrastructure.

7
The Poetry and Prose of Fisherfolk

There are few working lives more demanding than that of a fisherman; few working environments where one is more exposed to the vagaries of nature, from its most stern to its most peaceful. At sea, danger and frequently death are never all that far away; there is no time for frivolity when the nets are out and a gale is approaching. Fishing is a serious business, a fact which is reflected in much writing about the sea. In 'Crossing the Bar' Tennyson was not only expressing Victorian sentiments:

> *Twilight and evening bell,*
> *And after that the dark!*
> *And may there be no sadness of farewell,*
> *When I embark.*

In 'Old Fisherman with Guitar', Orcadian poet George Mackay Brown again brought his own experiences of the fishing life to the fore:

> *So fierce and sweet the song on the plucked string,*
> > *Know now for truth*
> *These hands have cut from the net*
> > *The strong*
> *Crab eaten corpse of Jock washed from a boat.*
> *One old winter, and gathered the mouth of Thora*
> > *to his mouth.*

Writers have long used turmoil at sea to instil fear into their readers. Stevenson, whose family built such light-houses as Skerryvore and the Bell Rock, could write from experience:

> *In the hollow bowels of the ship I hear the ponderous*
> *engines pant and trample. The basin gasps and baulks like*
> *an uneasy sleeper, and I hear the broad bows tilt with the*
> *big billows, and the hollow bosom boom against solid walls*
> *of water, and the great sprays scourge the deck . . . My heart*
> *beats and toils in the dark midparts of my body; like as the*
> *engine in the ship, my brain toils.*

'A Note at Sea'

Even William Topaz McGonagall has sought to terrify his readers as in 'John Rouat the Fisherman':

> *But still he clutched his oars, thinking to keep his cobble afloat,*
> *When one 'whelming billow struck heavily against the boat,*
> *And man and boat were engulfed in the briny wave,*
> *While the Storm Fiend did roar and madly did rave.*

But, enough of this sadness. The River Forth figures prominently in our verse and song in *Songs and Ballads of Scotland* by Hamish MacCunn. From the north side, John Ewen gives us the fine song, 'The Boatie Rows':

> *O weel may the boatie row, and better may she speed;*
> *O weel may the boatie row, that wins the bairnie's bread.*
> *The boatie rows, the boatie rows, the boatie rows fu' weel,*
> *And muckle luck attend the boat, the merlin and the creel.*
> *I cuist my line in Largo Bay, and fishes I caught nine;*
> *There's three to boil, and three to fry, and three to bait the line.*
> *The boatie rows, the boatie rows, the boatie rows indeed;*
> *And happy be the lot o' a' that wish the boatie speed.*

When we cross to the south side of the river, we enter the domain of Francis Collinson's 'Oyster Dredging Songs of the Forth':

> *Who'll dreg a buckie?*
> *I'll dreg a clam.*

I'll dreg a buckie,
And I'll be lucky
And I'll no be lang.

As has been pointed out earlier, such songs were made up largely on an impromptu basis. But there was never anything that suggested the impromptu when Robert Fergusson lifted his pen:

O' a' the waters that can hobble
A fishing yole or salmon cobble,
And can reward the fisher's trouble
      Or south or north
There's nane sae spacious and sae noble
      As Firth o' Forth.

In her the skate and codlin sail,
The eil fou souple wags her tail,
Wi' herrin, fleuk, and mackarel,
      And whytens dainty:
Their spindle shanks the labsters trail,
      Wi' partans plenty.

                    'Caller Oyster'

Most people would accept 'Caller Herrin' as the Forth's most famous fishing song. Lady Nairne who composed this gem gave the royalties from it to Nathaniel Gow to help him over a bad patch and there is reference to to the musician in one of its later verses which is seldom sung nowadays. Again though, in the song, the dangers inherent in the fishing life show through:

Wha'll buy my caller herrin'?
Oh ye may call them vulgar farin',
Wives and mithers maist despairin',
Ca' them lives o' men.

The wives and mothers who sold the fish from huge creels on their backs, also got a mention from a contemporary of Lady Nairne. Sir Walter Scott in his *Diary* of 1827 records:

*June 10 – Rose with the old consciousness of being free of
my daily task. I have heard the fish-women go to church of
a Sunday with their creels new washed, and a few stones in
them for ballast, just because they cannot walk steadily
without their usual load.*

Another diary entry of yesteryear casts an interesting aside
on the manners of the day. Boswell, in his *Journal of a Tour
of the Hebrides* in the company of his hero Dr Johnson,
comments:

*September 13th 1773 – During our sail, Dr Johnson
asked about the use of the dirk with which he imagined the
highlanders cut their meat. He was told, they had a knife
and fork besides, to eat with. He asked, 'how did the women
do?' and was answered, some of them had a knife and fork
too: but in general the men, when they had cut their meat,
handed their knives and forks to the women, and they
themselves eat with their fingers. The old tutor of
Macdonald always eat[s] fish with his fingers, alleging
the knife and fork gave it a bad taste. I took the liberty to
observe to Dr Johnson that he did so. 'Yes,' said he; 'but it
is because I am short-sighted, and afraid of bones, for
which reason I am not fond of eating many kinds of fish,
because I must use my fingers.*

Of all the fish in the sea, the herring is the one most sung
about. The 'Silver Darlings' brought out the muse in those
who wrought in their wake. Our folklore is so much richer
because of the lassies who followed the fishing fleet
around the country. A turn-of-the-century description of
the gutting comes from D.T. Holmes in his *Literary Tours of
the Highlands and Islands:*

*To Lerwick, during the fishing season, thousands of
women come from the Island of Lewis to gut the myriad
herring that are daily brought into the bay. There is an
extemporised town for the strangers on the outskirts,
over which may float many odours, weird, pungent and
unsavoury. All the processes of gutting, curing and*

*kippering go on in grand style. The women, clad in a kind
of oilskin, handle their dangerous implements in most
dexterous fashion. It is a horrid business but well paid.
Prolific nature is never tired of supplying these women with
work, for as many as 68,000 eggs have been found in the
roe of one female herring.*

Kipling had no compunctions about describing in detail
the bloody work of gutting at sea:

*. . . bringing one up with a finger under its gill and a finger
in its eye. He laid it on the edge of the pen; the knife-blade
glimmered with a sound of tearing, and the fish, slit from
throat to vent, with a nick on either side of the neck,
dropped at Long Jack's feet.*

*'Hi!' said Long Jack, with a scoop of his mittened hand.
The cod's liver dropped in the basket. Another wrench and
scoop sent the head and offal flying, and the empty fish slid
across to Uncle Salters, who snorted fiercely. There was
another sound of tearing, the backbone flew over the
bulwarks, and the fish, headless, gutted, and open,
splashed in the tub.*

Leaving the blood and guts behind and moving to the west
coast, D.T. Holmes in his *Literary Tours in The Highlands
and Islands of Shetland* introduced a note of history:

*Of course, Loch Fyne had a European reputation, which it
owed to its herring. The Popes of Rome used to eat these
herring in mediaeval times, and were sent them via
Amsterdam or Antwerp. Orthodox Catholics have always
had good judgement in the matter of fish, and especially the
French, who belong to a country which boasts of being the
eldest daughter of the Church. For many a generation
the French came annually to Lochgilphead and bartered
their kegs of claret for barrels of salt herring. The French
Revolution among its many effects, put a stop to this trade.
War lasted for so many years between Britain and France,
that, at the end of it all, the Continental sailors had
forgotten the way to Loch Fyne.*

Nor can it be said that for those wives that stayed at home, life was any more pleasant. Robert Louis Stevenson makes us feel her loneliness with 'I Sit Up Here at Midnight':

She raises herself on her elbow
And watches the firelit floor;
Her eyes are bright with terror,
Her heart beats fast and sore.

Beneath the roar of the flurries,
When the tempest holds its breath
She holds her breathing also –
It is all as still as death.

She can hear the cinders dropping,
The cat that purrs in its sleep –
The foolish fisher woman!
Her heart is on the deep.

If the herring figures prolifically in our poetry, prose and song, the same cannot be said about shellfish. The mind instinctively jumps first to Orcadian Allie Windwick's song 'Partans in his Creel' perhaps forgetting this is essentially a love story:

There's a peerie croft amang the heather, whar he says
*   we'll bide taegether;*
While he'll mak a living wae his boatie on the sea;
There's a wee bit hoose his faither bigget, stootly thatched
*   and snugly riggit,*
Waiting tae be taken ower by Willie an' by me!
Willie stands aroond and whistles; Willie's fields are fu' o'
*   thistles –*
Thistles never brought a body any milk and meal:
Na! I think I'd better tarry; bide a wee afore I marry –
No' till Willie catches mair than partans in his creel!

The few shellfish songs there are, do not sing the joys of crustacea-eating. Somehow, love-making seems to dominate even the work of gathering mussels for bait:

As I came in by Fisherrow Musselburgh was near me;
I threw off my mussel-pock and courted wi' my dearie.

'Fisherrow', Trad.

To be fair though to 'The Bonnie Fisher Lass', she was not
to be diverted by a suitor:

I stepped up beside her
And to her I did say,
'Why are you out so early,
Why are you going this way?'
She said, 'I'm going to look for bait,
Now allow me for to pass,
For our lines we must get ready'
Said the bonnie fisher lass.

'The Scottish Folk Singer', N.Buchan and P. Hall

In the early part of this century, Gavin Greig, a school-
master at New Deer and the Reverend James Duncan, the
minister at Lynturk near Alford, exerted themselves to the
full to produce the largest and most authentic collection of
Scottish folk-songs ever put together. Yet surprisingly, out
of the 1,200-odd songs in the collection, only sixty-eight
were to be placed in the nautical section. There was for a
time a school of thought that the pervading evangelical
hymns such as those of Moody and Sankey had dampened
the fishing folk-song tradition in the north-east of Scotland,
but later work by collector Harold George, the music
master at Banff Academy, and Hamish Henderson from the
School of Scottish Studies at Edinburgh University has
confirmed the existence of much other material. Those
with an interest in the poetry and prose of the fishing
grounds should also read the books of Peter Smith the
Cellardyke poet; 'Fit Like, Skipper?' by Peter Buchan; the
anthology *Glimmer of Cold Brine* published by Aberdeen
University Press; and George Ritchie's *The Real Price of Fish*
which covers the loss of 303 Aberdeen steam trawlers
between 1887 and 1961.

That those who respond to our need for fish still penetrate our thoughts is evident from the number of writers and poets who still turn to the topic for expression. Lillian Grant Rich's, 'Foghorn in the Night', says it all:

Ower and ower again
That warnin mane:
And though oot there at sea
I hae nae fishers o' my ain,
Dear lord, I prae sae fain –
Let me not ask in vain –
Bring oor boats safely hame.

Recipes

For far too long the Scots have been unadventurous in the preparation of their fish dishes. Perhaps this is understandable. One never tires of simply-prepared good fresh fish. To many of us there is little to compare with picking the flesh off a genuine Arbroath smokie or popping scallops into the mouth, straight from a few seconds under the grill. But here are a few recipes, both simple and slightly more so, that are worthy of appearance on the table, particularly if the occasion is special.

Suggestions for a first course

MOULES MARINIÈRE

2kg (4lbs) fresh mussels, washed and scrubbed
25g (1oz) butter or margarine
1 onion finely chopped
1 clove garlic, crushed
180ml (½ pint) dry white wine
30ml (2 tablespoons) lemon juice
3 bay leaves
salt and pepper
45ml (3 tablespoons) fresh chopped parsley

1. Melt the butter or margarine in a large saucepan and lightly cook the onion and garlic.

2. Add the liquids, bay leaves and seasonings, bring to the boil. Add the mussels. Cover and cook over a high heat, shaking the pan occasionally to ensure even cooking.

3. When all the mussels have opened (discard any that remain closed), transfer to a heated serving dish, reserving the liquid.

4. Return the liquid to the heat and boil rapidly until reduced by half; stir in the parsley.

5. Pour the sauce over the mussels and serve with French bread.

(Serves four)

TIMBALES

225g (8oz) smoked cod or whiting fillet,
fresh or defrosted, skinned and finely cubed
outer leaves of two leeks
15g (½oz) butter or nargarine, melted
125g (4oz) risotto rice
420ml (¾ pint) chicken or fish stock
(made with a half cube)
45ml (3 tablespoons) single cream
1 egg, beaten
black pepper

Preheat oven to 180°C/350°F, Gas Mark 4

1. Cut the leek leaves into strips, about 2.5cm (1") in width. Blanch for 2–3 minutes. Drain and cool under cold running water.

2. Lightly grease 6 ramekin dishes. Line with the leek leaves, leaving the ends overhanging the dishes.

3. Cook the rice in the stock for ten minutes, stirring occasionally, until the liquid is absorbed.

4. Stir in the fish, cream, egg and pepper. Spoon into the ramekin dishes. Fold over the leek leaves.

5. Cover and place the dishes into a large roasting tin half filled with hot water.

6. Cook for 25 minutes. Turn onto a serving plate and serve hot or cold.

(Serves six)

CULLEN SKINK

Surely, one of the world's great dishes. Can be a meal on its own.

450 g (1lb) Finnan haddock, fresh or defrosted
280ml (½ pint) water
2 onions, finely chopped
3 large potatoes, peeled and sliced
2.5ml (½ teaspoon) white pepper
420ml (¾ pint) milk
knob of butter
salt to taste
30ml (2 tablespoons) single cream
10ml (2 teaspoons) chopped parsley

1. Place haddock and water in a large saucepan and cook for 6–8 minutes over a gentle heat.

2. Drain fish and set aside. Strain the cooking liquid into a bowl, clean the saucepan and return strained liquid.

3. Add onions, potatoes and pepper, cook for approximately 20 minutes or until potatoes are tender.

4. Meanwhile, remove skin and bones from fish. Flake the flesh into a bowl.

5. When potatoes are cooked, remove pan from heat and mash the potatoes and onions in the liquid. Gradually add the milk.

6. Return to the heat, add the flaked fish, butter and season to taste, cook for 2–3 minutes stirring constantly until hot.

7. Add the cream and parsley just before serving.

(Serves four)

SCOTTISH MARITIME CHOWDER

This simple and quickly prepared soup should be a regular on the table. Much more elegant than the run-of-the-mill Continental fish soups.

450g (1lb) whiting fillets, fresh or defrosted,
skinned and cubed
175g (12oz) boneless Loch Fyne kippers, cubed
50g (2oz) unsmoked streaky bacon, de-rinded and chopped
225g (8oz) leeks, washed and thickly sliced
420ml (¾ pint) fish or chicken stock
280ml (½ pint) milk
salt and black pepper
chopped parsley to garnish

1. In a large saucepan cook the bacon until lightly browned.

2. Add the vegetables and stock, simmer for ten minutes.

3. Add the prepared fish and milk. Simmer for another 10 minutes until the fish and vegetables are tender.

4. Serve hot garnished with chopped parsley and accompanied by freshly made oatcakes.

(Serves four to six)

PRAWN BISQUE

Vies for honours with its more famous lobster bisque brother.

675g (1½ lbs) small, cooked, peeled,
warm water prawns, fresh or defrosted
15g (½ oz) butter
1 small onion, chopped
1 clove garlic, crushed
1 stick celery, chopped
140ml (¼ pint) dry white wine
560ml (1 pint) fish or chicken stock
5ml (1 teaspoon) tomato purée
1 bouquet garni
1 bay leaf
salt and pepper
140ml (¼ pint) single cream
30ml (2 tablespoons) brandy
paprika and chopped chives, to garnish

1. Melt the butter in a large pan. Cook onion, garlic and celery until soft.

2. Add wine, stock, tomato puree, bouquet garni, bay leaf and seasoning.

3. Simmer for 5–10 minutes to allow herbs to infuse.

4. Stir in the prawns, simmer for a further 3–5 minutes

5. Remove bouquet garni and bay leaf. Liquidise, return to the heat, simmer gently without boiling until piping hot and add the cream and brandy.

(Serves four to six)

Suggestions for a main course

SOLE WITH PRAWNS AND COURGETTES

4 lemon sole or plaice fillets, 175g (6oz),
fresh or defrosted, skinned
125g (4oz) cooked peeled prawns, fresh or defrosted
2 medium-sized courgettes, sliced
salt and pepper
15g (½ oz) butter or margarine
90ml (6 tablespoons) dry white wine or fish stock
2.5ml (½ teaspoon) paprika

1. In a small bowl mix the courgettes and prawns.

2. Lay the fillets onto a board, skinned side uppermost and season. Place a spoonful of filling on each fillet. Fold the fillets in half, dot with butter and place in a shallow pan.

3. Spoon over remaining filling and add the wine or fish stock.

4. Cover and cook gently over a low heat for 5–6 minutes.

5. Dust with paprika and serve with croquette potatoes.

(Serves four)

ISLE of SKYE FILOS

8 sheets filo pastry
sunflower oil, for brushing
45ml (3 tablespoons) reduced calorie mayonnaise
45ml (3 tablespoons) fromage frais
15ml (1 tablespoon) tomato ketchup
few drops Talisker whisky or Tabasco sauce
½ red pepper, finely chopped
375g (12oz) peeled prawns, fresh or defrosted
salt and black pepper

Preheat oven to 200°C/400°F, Gas Mark 6

1. Place four sheets of pastry, one on top of the other. Cut into six 10cm (4 inch) squares (approx.). Repeat for the remaining pastry.

2. Arrange four squares of pastry so that they overlap at an angle to give a pointed edge. Repeat eleven times with remaining squares.

3. Brush a twelve-hole patty tin with vegetable oil. Use arranged squares to line each hole.

4. Mix together remaining ingredients. Divide the filling between the filo cups. Bake for 10–15 minutes until pastry is golden brown.

(Makes twelve)

HIGHLAND FISH CREAM

450 (1lb) haddock fillets, fresh or defrosted, skinned
50g (2oz) fresh breadcrumbs
140ml (¼ pint) milk
50g (2oz) butter
salt and black pepper
2 eggs
30ml (2 tablespoons) single cream
280ml (½ pint) white sauce, flavoured with
parsley or shrimps

1. Finely chop the fish and add the breadcrumbs.

2. Heat the milk with the butter until the butter melts and pour over fish. Season with salt and pepper and leave to soak for ten minutes.

3. Beat one egg, separate the other and beat the yolk into the whole egg, whisk the egg-white until stiff. Stir the beaten egg into the fish mixture and fold the white in lightly with the cream.

4. Butter a mould or bowl and, if you like, dust with browned breadcrumbs. Pour in the mixture, cover with buttered greaseproof paper and tie down.

5. Steam in a pan with water covering halfway up the sides of the bowl for 40–45 miutes.

6. Turn out the fish mould and serve hot with the sauce.

(Serves four)

BREAD AND BUTTER SMOKED FISH PIE

175g (6oz) smoked cod or whiting fillet,
fresh or defrosted, skinned
50g (2oz) sweetcorn
1 buttered slice of bread quartered
1 egg
70ml (½ pint) semi-skimmed milk
5ml (1 teaspoon) fresh chopped parsley

Preheat oven to 180°C/350°F, Gas Mark 4.

1. Place the smoked fish and sweetcorn in an oven-proof dish.

2. Place the buttered bread on top of the fish, butter side up.

3. Beat together the egg, milk and parsley, pour over the mixture, soaking the bread well.

4. Bake for 30–35 minutes or until set and golden brown.

5. Serve with a selection of vegetables.

(Serves one)

HERRING WITH SPINACH AND PINE-NUTS

450g (1lb) herring fillets
15–20ml (1–2 tablespoons) sunflower or olive oil
1 small onion chopped
50g (2oz) frozen spinach, slightly thawed
50g (2oz) fresh breadcrumbs
25g (1oz) Parmesan cheese
salt and pepper
15g (½ oz) pine-nuts, lightly chopped

Preheat oven to 220°C/425°F, Gas Mark 7

1. Heat the oil in a pan, add the onion and cook for 2–3 minutes.

2. Add the spinach, breadcrumbs and cheese. Cook for one minute and set aside to cool.

3. Place each fillet onto a chopping board, skinned side down and season with salt and pepper.

4. Spoon the stuffing over each fillet, roll up and secure with a cocktail stick, if necessary.

5. Bake for 10–15 minutes, garnish with pine-nuts and serve with a green salad and ciabatta or pitta bread.

(Serves four)

SMOKY MACKEREL PENNE

450g (1lb) 'hot' smoked mackerel fillets,
skinned and cubed
15ml (1 tablespoon) sunflower oil
1 small onion, sliced
1 clove garlic, crushed
675g (1½ lbs) fresh tomatoes,
skinned and roughly chopped
30ml (2 tablespoons) chopped fresh basil
175g (6oz) pasta shapes, cooked
15ml (1 tablespoon) pumpkin seeds (optional)
basil leaf, to garnish

1. Heat the oil in a pan. Add the onions and garlic, cook until the onions are soft and transparent.

2. Stir in the tomatoes and basil. Cover and simmer for 1–2 minutes.

3. Add the fish and pasta, cook until piping hot. Spoon into individual oven-proof dishes.

4. Sprinkle over the pumpkin seeds. Garnish with basil and serve with crispy mixed lettuce.

(Serves four)

Tip: Kipper fillets can be substituted for the smoked mackerel fillets, simmer with the tomatoes for 5–6 minutes.

PIZZA PESCATORI

*175g (6oz) smoked haddock or cod fillet, fresh
or defrosted, skinned and cubed
15ml (1 tablespoon) tomato purée
one 18cm (7 inch) prepared pizza base
200g (7oz) can chopped tomatoes
2.5ml (½ teaspoon) dried oregano
black pepper
½ green pepper, de-seeded and sliced
1 small onion, thinly sliced
50g (2oz) Cheddar cheese, grated*

Preheat oven to 220°C/425°F, Gas Mark 7

1. Spread the tomato purée over the pizza base, top with the tomatoes and season with oregano and black pepper.

2. Add the green pepper, onion and fish. Sprinkle over the cheese.

3. Place the pizza onto a baking tray and cook for 15–20 minutes until golden brown.

4. Serve with baked potatoes and salad.

(Serves two)

SMOKED FISH ROULADE

450g (1lb) Finnan haddock
75g (3oz) flour
4 eggs, separated
30ml (2 tablespoons) water
25g (1oz) Parmesan cheese, grated
black pepper
25g (1oz) unsalted butter
160ml (7 fl oz) milk
15ml(1 tablespoon) chopped fresh parsley

Preheat oven to 200°C/400°F, Gas Mark 6

1. Poach the fish in ¾–1 pint water for 10 minutes. Cool, skin and flake. Grease and line a 30 by 20 cm (12" by 8") swiss roll tin.

2. Sift 50g (2oz) of the flour into a bowl. Beat in the egg yolks and water until smooth. Stir in the cheese and pepper.

3. In a separate bowl, whisk the egg whites until stiff. Fold into the mixture and pour into the prepared tin. Spread the mixture evenly and bake for 12–15 minutes until risen and golden brown.

4. To make the filling: melt the butter in a pan, stir in the remaining flour and cook for one minute. Remove from the heat, gradually stir in the milk.

5. Return to the heat and cook, stirring until thickened. Fold in the cooked fish and parsley and season with pepper.

6. Turn the roulade onto greaseproof paper, trim the edges. Spread over the filling and roll up. Cut into slices and serve.

(Serves four)

PRAWN AND SPINACH BAKE

225g (8oz) small, cooked, peeled, cold-water prawns,
fresh or defrosted
15g (½ oz) butter
1 clove garlic, crushed
450g (1lb) fresh spinach, trimmed and washed
pinch nutmeg
275g (10oz) potatoes

Sauce:
25g (1oz) butter
25g (1oz) flour
280ml (½ pint milk)
125g (4oz) cheese, grated

Preheat oven to 190°C/375°F, Gas Mark 5

1. Melt the butter in a large pan, add the garlic, spinach and nutmeg and cook for 1–2 minutes.

2. Cover the base of a large shallow dish with spinach mixture. Top with prawns.

3. Meanwhile to make the sauce – melt the butter in a saucepan, add the flour and cook for one minute. Remove from the heat, gradually blend in the milk. Return to the heat and bring to the boil, stirring all the time. Cook for 2–3 minutes. Add 75g (3oz) of the cheese and stir until it melts.

4. Pour the sauce over prawns. Top with sliced potatoes and sprinkle on remaining cheese.

5. Bake in oven for twenty minutes until golden brown.

6. Serve with sliced tomato and green salad.

(Serves four)

KIPPER CAKES

450g (1lb) kipper fillets, fresh or defrosted, skinned
1 egg, beaten
dash Worcestershire sauce
175g (6oz) fresh breadcrumbs

1. Place the kipper fillets into a food processor or blender. Process or blend until finely flaked.

2. Stir in the egg, Worcestershire sauce and breadcrumbs.

3. Divide the mixture into 8 pieces and shape into 5cm (2") rounds. Chill for 10–15 minutes.

4. Cook under a low grill for 8–10 minutes turning once. Serve with salad and tomato or onion relish.

(Serves four)